the happy introvert

the happy introvert

a wild and crazy guide for celebrating your true self

ELIZABETH WAGELE

Ulysses Press

Published by: Ulysses Press
P.O. Box 3440
Berkeley, CA 94703
www.ulyssespress.com

ISBN10: 1-56975-546-9
ISBN13: 978-1-56975-546-4
Library of Congress Control Number: 2006900288

Printed in the United States of America by Bang Printing

10 9 8 7 6 5 4 3 2

Managing Editor: Claire Chun
Editor: Lily Chou
Production: Matt Orendorff, Lisa Kester
Cover design: Matt Orendorff
Index: Sayre Van Young
Cover photography: © Royalty-Free/Corbis (front); © Photos.com (back)

Distributed by Publishers Group West

To my family and friends.
To understanding and acceptance.

Contents

1

The Introvert in an Extraverted World

Eastern cultures see introversion as a value and give it much esteem. Western cultures prefer extraversion. For a balanced, safe, and caring world, we must learn to value both.
—*John Weber*

The other day, I heard a news anchor on a major TV network disdainfully refer to a bad guy who's been in the news a lot recently as "a recluse and an introverted nut case." The juxtaposition of the words "introverted" and "nut case" really pushed my buttons since I'm an introvert myself. The first time I felt sensitive about this was as a teenager having a discussion with my mother. When

I casually and proudly referred to myself as an introvert, she shot back angrily, "You are not! You're a nice girl!"

It wasn't long before I realized there were others besides my mother for whom "introvert" had a negative meaning. A headline in a popular magazine, for example, erroneously claimed that the most important ingredient for happiness is to *not* be an introvert. I strongly disagree. The rich inner lives we introverts lead enable us to feel comfortable with ourselves and to be interesting to our friends. Some of the most brilliant, creative, and productive humans in history (Einstein, Jane Austen, Beethoven, Michelangelo, Isaac Newton, and Howard Hughes, for example) were introverts.

Each of us uses both introversion and extraversion in our daily lives, but our personalities are characterized by one of these attitudes more than the other. This is probably the most important personality difference there is. Both types have social needs, but some introverts, like whales, can be alone for weeks before needing to come together with other beings. Extraverts usually need to connect more frequently and have a larger amount of friends and acquaintances.

While it's true that some of us introverts can be hard to get to know, being quiet, or even reclusive, at times doesn't make us aliens or weirdos. Besides, is this any worse than those overly gregarious people who are "on stage" all the time?

Introverts and extraverts often excel in different areas, so we *could* help each other out . . .

. . . but instead, many unnecessary misunderstandings, some irreversible, occur between us every day.

I called this book *The Happy Introvert* to dispel the belief that to be an introvert means you are a victim of depression or another unhappy state. I wanted to set the record straight before anyone cracked open the book. Yes, we introverts can be happy. We experience the usual range of human feelings, including joy and contentment. Our values are somewhat different from extraverts', however. We excel in the kind of happiness which compels us to develop skills and knowledge that will sustain a rich inner life.

If you're an introvert, you may feel relieved that someone knows an introvert is capable of this kind of contentment.

> I love being thought of as a happy introvert. Being alone is always relaxing for me. I am quite social for an introvert, but it always feels good when events are over and I can digest them alone. —*Jim Campbell*

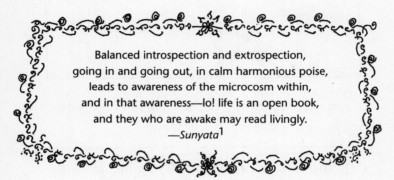

Balanced introspection and extrospection,
going in and going out, in calm harmonious poise,
leads to awareness of the microcosm within,
and in that awareness—lo! life is an open book,
and they who are awake may read livingly.
—*Sunyata*[1]

Why It's Important to Learn about Personality Differences

Parents and teachers can use their knowledge about personality differences to work with children's learning styles and allow their true personalities to unfold. Employers can run more efficient businesses by giving introverts the privacy we need and assigning extraverts jobs that allow them to use their people skills. Adolescents' self-regard and self-esteem improve when they learn that introversion and extraversion are equally legitimate human attributes.

On an individual level, studying your introverted and extraverted attitudes will help you value your strengths and become more realistic about your limitations. The prevailing view is that

being moral means to be in harmony with the group: "You are suspect if you don't go along." This makes such an emotional impact
on introverts that many of us fool ourselves into thinking we, too,
are extraverts. But not accepting one's true nature creates stress. I
used to force myself to attend events I didn't enjoy. When I finally
realized I didn't need to suffer through certain kinds of social functions, I stopped going to them and devoted more time to activities I
liked.

About This Book

First, this book celebrates the richness we introverts experience in
our inner worlds, and acknowledges that these experiences can
be exported for others to enjoy if we choose. Practical suggestions
help us introverts become even happier by learning to negotiate
the extraverted world and stand up for ourselves and each other.

Second, regardless of where the parts of your personality fall
on the introversion/extraversion continuum, you'll find information here for getting along more smoothly with the introverts in
your life.

Chapter 5 is important for adding to your life through the introverted process and creativity.

Notice if some of my cartoons bring a smile to your face—
they're speaking in an introverted way, from a happy place in me
to a happy place in you.

Introverts and Extraverts

When we look at introversion/extraversion as two aspects of the
same person, the inner ("intro") part mostly refers to perceiving,
thinking, imagining, conceiving, and reflecting. The outer
("extra") part is mostly concerned with the parts of our lives
where we socialize, network, reach out, and get things done.

Text continued on page 16.

ARE YOU AN INTROVERT?

Note how many of these statements you agree with:

1. You usually like being with people (not too many at once) for no longer than an hour or two at a time.
2. In group discussions, the topic being discussed sometimes changes by the time you have collected your thoughts and are ready to speak.
3. People sometimes realize you are interesting only after they get to know you.
4. You dislike being asked broad, sweeping questions—especially by strangers.
5. You are critical of superficiality.
6. You sometimes procrastinate when you want to avoid interacting with people.
7. You like to concentrate in depth when doing a project.
8. You are often content to be alone with your thoughts, feelings, and activities.
9. Your style of speech tends to be calm and quiet.
10. You often prefer that others make reservations, announcements, phone calls, and introductions.
11. You may be more likely to engage in learning or improving your skills than to look for outside stimulation.
12. Your ability to remember people's names is average to low.
13. You can be yourself much more easily if you feel at ease with someone.
14. In social situations, you sometimes stand back and observe.

If most of the above statements apply to you, you are probably an introvert.

ARE YOU AN EXTRAVERT?

Note how many of these statements you agree with:

1. You generally prefer being with others or talking on the phone to being alone.
2. You have a lot of energy.
3. Your voice is usually strong and confident and you speak with little or no hesitation.
4. Some people appear to see you as being on a power trip, artificially optimistic, or overly dramatic.
5. You tend to think out loud, so what you say isn't always fully thought out.
6. In general, you are fast more than accurate.
7. You notice the latest styles and pay much attention to the way you look.
8. You frequently seek companionship or other outside stimulation.
9. You enjoy shopping and like to buy on impulse.
10. You prefer a busy environment when working or studying.
11. You want to make an impact on your community, whether school, job, church, or neighborhood.
12. Connecting with others requires little or no effort on your part.
13. You become impatient when the people you are with engage in soul searching.
14. You dislike tasks that take a long time to complete.

If most of the above statements apply to you, you are probably an extravert.

See the Appendix on page 166 for more characteristics of introverts and extraverts.

. . . An introvert goes to be alone by the lake, finds a seat, gets comfortable, and realizes when a dog comes by that she had been there for 30 minutes lost in her own thoughts. The lake has been a background to this deep introverting. Extraverts go to the lake to be alone and will most likely walk around it first, then on sitting down will be in touch with the whole setting, notice the beach house and the birds that fly by. They will see the dog coming from a mile off and will be much more in touch with the outer and much less in touch with the inner processes in the same half-hour. —*Anne Brennan*[2]

Introverts make up only 25 to 30 percent of the U.S. population.[3] Some of us feel separate from the extraverted majority and the mainstream culture. We tend to be individualistic, keep to ourselves, and feel distanced, even from each other. For certain extreme introverts, being around people can be a negative experience:

. . . I go into solitude, so as not to drink out of everybody's cistern. When I am among the many I live as the many do, and I do not think I really think; after a time it always seems as if they want to banish myself from myself and rob me of my soul. —*Friedrich Nietzsche*

Extraverts' tendencies to focus outward and want to be shakers, movers, and doers are highly valued in Western society. One famous extravert, Pablo Picasso, was powerful and competitive, made a strong impression on others, and revolutionized the world of art. Dramatic and outspoken by nature, extraverts radiate excitement, are often impulsive, bold, and venturesome, and usually gravitate toward people whether they've met them before or not. They value making an impact on their community and excel at self-promotion and persuading others to help them out.

Following are some examples of both introverts and extraverts:

- When extraverted Spike attends social functions, words tumble out of his mouth easily and he introduces many of the topics discussed. He almost always makes new friends and leaves feeling energized.

- I asked a few friends what they thought I should do when I was invited to a weeklong symposium with 20 people I didn't know. The extraverts said, "Go!" The introverts suggested I stay home and not drain myself.

> Yes, it's true I have a full plate, but I can always do more. I'm always looking for excitement—something to make the adrenaline rush. Better to be overworked than bored.
> —*Manny Glaser, an extravert*

- Bertha and Terry have an introverted son who thrives on solitude and an extraverted son who thrives on people. When they were home from college for two weeks last Christmas, the introverted one kept to himself until the last day, then phoned a few friends. His extraverted brother spent almost every minute socializing.

Text continued on page 20.

AN INTROVERT'S POEM

Introverts are like treasures of the seas,

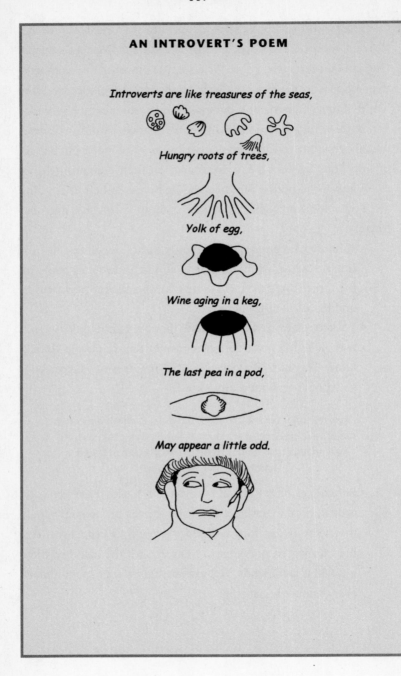

Hungry roots of trees,

Yolk of egg,

Wine aging in a keg,

The last pea in a pod,

May appear a little odd.

Justin

- Tyler, a professional football player, celebrates in an introverted way when he scores a touchdown. He acts as though nothing has happened. On the other hand, his teammate Justin celebrates in an extraverted way by strutting around proudly in the end zone.

Tyler

- While some introverts have strong, decisive personalities, in general we're not as assertive as most extraverts. Tamar often waits to speak up until she's 100 percent sure she's right or tends to nudge and persevere instead of using obvious force.

- Manny, a competitive, extraverted businessman, is 75 and retired. "The desire to do so many things is there but the energy is lacking," he told me. "Being active in worthwhile intellectual activities drives away my feelings of loneliness, but I worry that I'm not communicating with the rest of the world."

In the Beginning

Beginning in infancy, most introverts' senses are easily overwhelmed, so introverted children tend to be more comfortable observing from a distance. As they mature, they may *want* to interact, but they might encounter challenges, having had less practice making entrances and sustaining conversations than most of their peers.

Some young introverts would rather play by themselves because it's more comfortable. Others *do* feel comfortable socially, but simply prefer playing alone.

Extraverts' inborn temperaments are relatively sturdy. They usually regard being with others as exciting and pleasurable, engage in attention-getting activities with few or no ill affects, and prefer *not* to be alone.

Mental Processes

> When in my life minor problems arose, I always went
> within for the answer. I never reached out
> to others for what I should or should not do.
> —*Sunyata, an introvert*[4]

Introverts only fully grasp events, objects, and situations after we have taken the material from the outside, chewed it up, and mixed it with our psychic being. Until this process is complete, usually without knowing it, we may not know how we feel or what we want and our behavior may be passive or ambivalent.

Introverts reflect on new information at length and react relatively slowly.

Extraverts are geared more for action, so they reflect and react almost at the same time.

By the time we have finished processing information, however, our opinions are firm and we hold on to them tenaciously.

Extraverts' short reflecting time sometimes results in impulsive, disruptive behavior. Introverts, however, often keep their emotions bottled up while they reflect upon their experiences, then reflect upon their reflections, and so on. Until an experience is well integrated into the context of other thoughts, feelings, and impressions, introverts may feel confused, unsure, and not quite present:

> Once I was walking down the street with Carolyn when a mutual friend came toward us looking upset. Carolyn, an extravert, ran up to her, gave her a big hug, and exclaimed with all her heart, "You poor thing. It's going to be alright!" I wish I could reach out like that to help people feel better, but it's very hard for an introvert to act quickly with so little information. I would've had to go home and mull it over a few hours, then give our friend a call and probe cautiously to determine if she really needed my help. I concluded that both introverts and extraverts are necessary to have around—introverts to look at a situation in depth and extraverts to take matters in hand when spontaneity is needed. —*Karen McArdle, an introvert*

Taking the time we need to make decisions is sometimes embarrassing and uncomfortable for introverts. Acting in haste, however, may not reflect our true thoughts or feelings and can therefore be a mistake.

REVERSING DIRECTION

When we introverts need to satisfy curiosity and relationship needs, the direction of our attention reverses from inward to outward. Extraverts reverse attention from outward to inward when it's necessary to ponder. The following examples illustrate this occurrence.

An outer-directed pianist impressed audiences with his technical skill. When he was forced into a ten-year political exile, restricted to playing only for himself, he began to listen more to the music than to the response of the audience. His sensitivity toward what he was playing increased and his interest in presenting an image faded. Eventually, he became one of the greatest music interpreters of his time.

Andy was a reserved and observant child who hardly spoke until high school, when the flow of his psychic energy reversed from inward to outward and he became sociable and talkative. It wasn't a difficult transition, he claims, because he had many extraverted role models among his friends and family. As an adult, Andy now spends some of his time immersed in philosophy and the rest as a real estate consultant. He feels more peaceful and authentic in his inward moments.

Katya, a writer and musician, believes she is equally introverted and extraverted. Her extraverted periods are most fulfilling when she is able to communicate successfully and her periods of introversion tend to alternate between feeling creative and positive and disconnected and withdrawn.

Mahatma Gandhi, whose strong sense of idealism and asceticism was combined with the ability to bring about enormous change in the world, almost defies typing. As a young man, he had a career as an attorney. Later, he organized boycotts and en-

gaged in non-violent disobedience. As India's most notable activist and political leader, he improved the status of Hindu Untouchables, freed India from the British, and helped revive native industries. Gandhi wore the loincloth of the lowliest Indian, gave up all possessions, and lived a spiritual life of prayer, fasting, and meditation. At the time of his death, many Indians considered him a saint.

Social Preferences

As soon as he was alone, Andrey Yefimitsch abandoned himself to a feeling of relief. How pleasant to lie motionless on the sofa and to know that one is alone in the room! Real happiness is impossible without solitude. The fallen angel betrayed God probably because he longed for solitude, of which the angels knew nothing.
—from Ward No. 6 by Anton Chekhov

Extraverts are drawn to outside sources of stimulation. Being alone, or the threat of being alone, can frighten them. For example, extraverted Julie isn't interested in her internal world or in hearing about mine. She prefers to talk about the latest party she attended, her social dancing lessons, or how she is expanding her dining room to hold more guests. Extraverted Norris also keeps

Extraverts can be misfits, too.

busy trying to avoid a social vacuum. Drawing attention to himself is a defense mechanism against anxiety, he says. "Doing something keeps me intact. I don't have the courage to shut up."

Brewster, an unmistakable extravert, exhibits typically outgoing behavior. He had shattered his leg in a neighborhood football game and was waiting in a wheelchair to see a doctor. Shortly after I arrived, he suddenly interrupted a joke he was telling and angrily called out, to no one in particular, "Get me a better wheelchair—one with a leg rest! I'm hurting!" and persisted until someone brought him one. With his leg more comfortable, he began to tell us, individually and collectively, about how the injury took place, which TV shows he liked, and what he was going to eat when he got home. When he was called in to see the doctor, his roomful of new friends said good-bye to him almost in unison. You would have thought we were his 20 closest relatives.

In quiet solitude, we introverts trust our own sense of reality and feel protected from the harsh and puzzling aspects of the outer world. Our thoughts turn to other people somewhat less than extraverts' thoughts might.

When people tend to measure things by external standards, they look outside themselves for guidance and may see personal interpretations as wrong. They occasionally look within, but don't stay there long. For one thing, too much input from their subjective world might interfere with their ability to take action.

Recently, I got off an elevator, absorbed in thought, when an outgoing woman getting in said, "What a surprise to find the elevator almost empty at this time of day!" She looked at me with wide eyes and a big smile, demanding a response, I thought, that would satisfy her need to connect with another human being. I felt anxious and annoyed that I was being forced into what seemed to me a superficial exchange of words, and could think of nothing to say. Just then, the extraverted friend I had come to meet arrived and the two of them, who had never met, began chatting together effortlessly and gracefully.

SHYNESS

To be shy means to be cautious, timid, or mistrustful of other people. Shyness affects more introverts than extraverts and is usually caused by a mixture of genes and the effects of our social

environment during childhood. Shy children are more vigilant than others and tend to have higher-than-normal heart rates and blood pressure. Harry, an adult I know, is shy unless he is representing or defending someone else. Martha is normally shy, too, though at work she makes quick decisions and presents her opinions confidently. Shy people tend to be ill at ease, nervous, and sometimes shut down around people.

Catalysts, however, can make a difference:

> My introverted mother was not a loud person, but she attracted (even encouraged) loudness and laughter. Just as she was the perfect party piano player, creating a mood for others to be the lives of the party, she was the perfect social companion, creating a mood for others (such as myself) to come to life. — *John Boe, an introvert*[5]

Shy people are often understanding and compassionate. For example, even though Princess Diana of England was naturally shy, she adjusted to public life and used her fame to promote causes such as raising AIDS awareness, eradicating land mines, and helping the homeless.

Extraverts sometimes feel shy, too, but this is more likely to be temporary.

SOCIAL PHOBIA

In this extreme form of shyness, which is believed to have both biological and environmental causes, contact with others results in dread and panic. Social phobics usually want some attention but are afraid they'll suffer humiliation if the spotlight is

turned on them. Most are introverts, but extraverts can also have this problem. Doctors treat severe cases with talk therapy or psychotherapy, which is thought to be more useful in the long run, and/or medication.

I wonder if social phobics who are highly extraverted are slightly more frustrated and miserable than introverted ones.

How to Tell Introverts from Extraverts

> Social convention has little meaning for me—
> I don't know how to lock my mind on to a trend and
> wouldn't want to. If an experience is going to mean
> anything to me, it must touch me deep inside.
> —*Gus Wagele, an introvert*

We introverts tend to feel at home inside ourselves whether thinking, feeling, or experiencing periods of emptiness. Our private worlds can be a source of joy, solace, sorrow, and entertainment. We *might* conclude that people who spend long periods of time alone are introverts. But if making an impact on the outside world is foremost in their thoughts and dreams, they might be extraverts.

Identifying introverts when they're playing roles, such as host, guide, teacher, or performer, can be difficult. In grammar school, Miranda would put on lively and dramatic acting performances, but after the play was over she would go back to being her naturally quiet self. Just because people perform doesn't mean they are extraverts. Introverted comedians, Steve Martin, Rowan Atkins ("Mr. Bean"), and Ellen deGeneres, for example, often have unique or wacky points of view and hide behind masks or exaggerated roles. The styles of Bill Cosby, Rosie O'Donnell and Jay Leno, however, are more conversational and sociable, and point to extraversion.

Introverts may shun newness. Their most cherished experiences tend to deepen with repetition; they might see their favorite movie over and over, for example, or go back to the same forest year after year. Extraverts' enjoyment is more likely to come from variety and participating with others.

Introverts become especially intense and persuasive when their deepest values are threatened. When upset, they tend to feel inadequate, anxious, and/or apathetic, while upset extraverts tend to feel hysterical or manic. Some introverts talk constantly when with people because they feel nervous when they socialize.

> . . . How different "fiery" [extraverted] Laertes is
> [from introverted Hamlet]. When his father, Polonius,
> is murdered, he quickly returns from France, raises a
> rebellious mob, and assaults the palace. How easy it would be
> for Hamlet, loved of the people, to raise a similar rebellion,
> to oust the murderer of the rightful king with a coup. But
> Hamlet never considers such a politically sophisticated and
> ambitious act. Instead he soliloquizes, meditates, waits.
> —John Boe[6]

How Introverts and Extraverts Interpret Each Other

> Introverts are not sure the world will understand them.
> For this and other reasons, they often proceed slowly
> and cautiously and their behavior is sometimes
> misunderstood as waffling, passive, or pessimistic.
> —*Carolyn Dahlgren Rhodes*

Some extraverts feel the relaxed pace and inner strength of their introverted friends balances their own extraverted tendencies. More often, however, extraverts are attracted to other extraverts, whose energy matches their own. Some extraverts simply overlook introverts; others associate the quieter world of introversion with depression, emptiness, or the abyss; still others think introverts are trying to be like them but not doing a good job of it. One extravert complains that introverts are "too careful, too cautious, and not alive enough."

> We spend so much time thinking about things like the
> meaning of life and death and how complicated everything
> is. . . . Since many do not enjoy thinking about such things,
> they assume we must be unhappy doing all that pondering.

> And we certainly don't get any happier having them
> tell us we're unhappy (by their definition of happy).
> —*Elaine N. Aron, an introvert, author of* Highly Sensitive People[7]

This psychologist sees shy people as losers and encourages her readers to act in a way that would make most introverts cringe:

> . . . In another of Dr. Kassorla's books, *Go For It!* she divides people into two categories, "winners," who get what they want through aggressive self-promotion, and "losers," whose modesty, shyness, and aversion to confrontation keep them from succeeding. To win, one must learn to give extravagant praise and "full attention," to smile constantly, to declare one's love openly, and to "brag, boast, and broadcast" in order to make a "dynamic first impression." —*Jane Mayer, on Monica Lewinsky's psychologist*[8]

When we introverts see extraverts engaging in extreme smiling, bounce, and bravado, we often think they are insincere. In Western countries especially, extraverts often see quiet introverts as depressed, angry, or snobbish; it might be different if introversion were the norm.

Some extraverts are grumpy by nature, but since our culture pushes us to act as though we have no problems, many of them, and some introverts, too, try to show a happy exterior regardless of how they feel inside.

It is often difficult to know whether a quiet person is expressing a natural preference for introversion, is in a temporary mood, has been frightened into withdrawal, or a combination.

ARE INTROVERTS THE ONLY NUT CASES?

Extraverts can be bad guys as much as introverts, but the news media was shocked when they discovered that a German teenager, who had committed a horrendous crime, was talkative, spoke loudly, liked parties, and was always surrounded by friends. We introverts, with our tendencies to be quiet, thoughtful, and nonconforming, represent our culture's shadow and are almost *expected* to engage in deviant behavior. I doubt the fact that we're not as unhappy as they think we are will make it to the front page, but I think people will change their minds about us . . . in time.

Getting Along in an Extraverted World

In order to stay happy, take responsibility for how others see and understand you. Let people know if you don't want to have a conversation while the television is on, for example. We introverts need a certain amount of attention, of course, yet we often don't ask to be noticed. If you feel neglected, try to determine if you've been overlooked rather than shunned. Some introverts "see" themselves as invisible, but we may be more important to others than we think. As an exercise, draw some family scenes and prominently include yourself.

Learn to regard being shy, if you are, as an inborn tendency—it's not a character flaw. When you participate in social occasions that are difficult for you, appreciate yourself for step-

QUIZ ON CHAPTER ONE

(Answer T for "true" and F for "false")

1. People are either 100% introverted or 100% extraverted.
2. Introverts tend to sacrifice breadth for depth, while extraverts tend to sacrifice depth for breadth.
3. Introverts have all the patience in the world for people who don't dig down deep for answers.
4. Some introverts' inner knowing is nonverbal, so they have trouble describing themselves and putting their thoughts into words.
5. Introverts don't respond to *others'* inner worlds.
6. Some people, even other introverts, think of introverts as aloof, inscrutable, and self-involved.
7. Extraverts tend to be outgoing consistently, while introverts are only outgoing when comfortable.
8. If you want to measure your introversion/extraversion and some other personality traits, you can take the MBTI test (Myers-Briggs Type Indicator).
9. Of the nine personality types in the Enneagram system, the 4, 5, and 9, often called the Romantic, the Observer, and the Peacemaker, tend to be the most introverted.
10. Introverts are fond of being intruded upon and love to conform.

ANSWERS:
1. false; 2. true; 3. false; 4. true; 5. false; 6. true; 7. true; 8. true; 9. true; 10. false

ping out of your comfort zone, as is evidenced in the following story. Introverted Diane is a philosophy professor (most philosophers are introverts) who works hard to be sociable at faculty parties. Instead of going home exhausted and depressed, as she did in her teens, she now pats herself on the back for having taken on the challenge. Extraverts deserve credit, as well, for slowing down and engaging in introspection.

Accept yourself if you don't respond with socially perfect comments on every occasion. While you might wish you were as spontaneous as some extraverts you know, you are less likely to put your foot in your mouth. Some introverts deliver lectures rather than participating in conversations. You can tell by the lack of responses you receive. If this applies to you, try to take more of an interest in what others have to say.

You may want to avoid speaking in public, but if you want to improve this skill, join a group like Toastmasters to practice and learn techniques. If you *want* to take part in conversations and activities but feel uncomfortable, seek counseling.

2
Relationships

Observing yourself in a relationship is invaluable for both the relationship and your self-knowledge. Most introverts have a head start at being good observers. Other ingredients for a successful relationship, in addition to self-knowledge, include stability, contentment, compassion, independence, and the willingness to discuss what's going on between you. The ability most introverts have to not need constant companionship is also invaluable in the context of marriage and friendships.

> In relationships, *introverts* can discover
> they are different from the construct of
> themselves they have in their minds.
> *Extraverts* can learn that, regardless of the image
> they try to project, they <u>do</u> have a core
> and it <u>is</u> experienced by the other.

Friends, relatives, and partners can think of many reasons why they shouldn't talk about their relationship, such as avoiding arguments or not wanting to hurt the other or take a risk. Discussing personality differences, however, is a helpful way to start improving communication and making other improvements.

IN RELATIONSHIPS, DO YOU BEHAVE MORE LIKE AN INTROVERT OR AN EXTRAVERT?

Note which statement in each pair you are more likely to say (or want to say) to your partner, friend, or coworker:

1. "Stop rushing me."   "Hurry up."

2. "I want to stay home."   "Let's go to a party."

3. "I want to improve myself."   "I want to change the world."

4. "Let's explore this in depth."   "Let's see what the next item is."

5. "Thanks for keeping the conversation going."   "Thanks for your original thoughts."

6. "I need to think about it."   "We need to talk about it."

7. "Give me more privacy."   "Don't retreat."

8. "You overwhelm me."   "I can't get a reaction out of you."

9. "I admire your dynamism."   "I admire your steadiness."

10. "Let's do less."   "Let's do more."

11. "Okay, but let's not stay long."   "Why do you always want to leave so early?"

12. "Don't intrude."   "A penny for your thoughts."

13. "I'll read up on it."   "I'll ask around."

14. "I'll think about it."   "I'll know what I think when I say it."

If you checked more items on the left, you play a relatively introverted role in relationships. Items on the right indicate a more extraverted role.

Paired introverts usually respect each other's privacy, engage in separate activities side by side, and have focused discussions. Two "feeling types" tend to soul-search, while two "thinking types" tend to share on a more intellectual or informational level. Sometimes introvert/introvert couples insulate themselves from people outside the relationship and may neglect discussing problems in order to avoid confrontation.

Two introverts

We listen to Bach, Brahms, and Bartok
and go for drives in the rain.
—*An introverted couple*

Sometimes it's hard to make new friends. They're so . . . new.
—*An introvert*

I am most drawn to the world inside all of our minds,
which is just as broad and rich as the extraverted world.
Part of what is interesting about e-mail and Internet discussion
groups is that they are building railroads for people to travel
in the Inner World—they link introverts together.
We can communicate just as much as extraverts can,
but there's a different feel to it—a different rhythm.
—*Nigel Thompson, an introvert*

Paired extraverts share thoughts, feelings, and activities and often have a household busy with friends coming and going. Sometimes extravert/extravert couples are too busy to have sufficient time for each other, feel they don't get listened to enough, or compete for attention and power.

Two extraverts

When two introverts or two extraverts become partners, one usually assumes a more introverted role and the other a more extraverted one.

Introverts who have extraverted partners often feel pressured to participate in small talk and to react spontaneously and enthusiastically. They may sense their extraverted partner is critical of them for lacking social skills. Introverted Michael, however, appreciates his extraverted wife's openness with people. When they met, he was fearful of social situations and Gail was his entry into conversations. Little by little, he learned from her to join in on his own. She learned from his example to pay more attention to her quiet side.

On the flip side, introverted Nigel becomes frustrated at his extraverted friends' slowness when it comes to internal processing, such as grasping metaphors and meanings in movies. He claims that people find *him* "abysmally slow and frustrating," however, when it comes to external processes such as preparing schedules, getting packed, decorating, and so on.

But not all relationships work out. Introverted Nick enjoyed the camaraderie of the other men—all extraverts—in his poker group. Seeing them one evening a month was just right. He had belonged to the group for about two years when they went on a weekend outing to a cabin. This turned out to be too much companionship for him, as he had suspected. The other men had so much fun, however, they decided the earnings from future games would be set aside to finance more trips. When Nick complained about contributing to weekends he wouldn't be attending, the others responded sarcastically and laughed at him for not wanting to participate in their "meaningful bonding experiences." Since he was no longer having fun, Nick quit going to the poker games. Years later, he thought about how his experience would have been if his poker buddies had known type theory. He might have told them at the outset, "I won't be going to the weekend. I'm an introvert," knowing they'd understand.

Extraverts who have introverted partners may sense their partner is critical of them for fearing their own inner worlds, worrying about being left alone with insufficient stimulation, or being easily swayed by trends and fads. Such a partnership can work, however, as in extraverted Shirley's case. When Shirley wanted to have an exchange student live with her family, her husband and children, all introverts, made it clear that they would be miserable with a stranger in the house. In order to satisfy her desire for more people in her life, she became more involved in community activities.

Introverts in Relationships

In order to communicate, we introverts must translate our always-changing thoughts, feelings, impressions, and reactions into a language that others, whether they be extraverts or other introverts, can understand. Sometimes this is easy and effortless, but

often it takes an enormous amount of energy. When slow, it can be way too slow for our companion. Ed Mooney realized this:

> I used to carpool with a friend who couldn't stand how slow I was to respond when I was searching for the right word to convey a subtlety. She'd finish my sentences, which would drive me nuts because she finished them with words I'd NEVER say. So, as the intonation of her voice rose, as if to ask, in effect, "Isn't that what you were searching for?" I'd have to always say NO! and try to continue the thought my own way. She didn't get the point, so after one year we just stopped carpooling.

Ideally, we can talk about these things, explain that our processing takes time and can't be rushed, and ask for patience. Of course, it doesn't always work out this way.

How to Get Along with Introverts

Since extraverts tend to be exuberant and enthusiastic, they sometimes feel like a bull—or at least a calf—in a china shop around introverts. "Must we always restrain ourselves in order to not offend?" they might ask. We all want to feel free to be ourselves, but relationships run more smoothly when we're aware of one another's needs and sensitivities. The following suggestions are intended for both introverts and extraverts:

- Ask if now is a good time to talk instead of taking it for granted that introverts want to have a conversation.

- Unless you ask some clarifying questions, you often can't tell whether introverts are worried about something, involved in their own thoughts, or want to be left alone.

- Help introverts feel relaxed and safe, and show an interest in *their* world.

- Treat introverts gently—loud or dramatic expressions of emotion may frighten them. Your point of view will come across better through gentle persistence than if you come on strongly or put them on the spot.

- Think of creative solutions if pacing is a problem. Elaine Chernoff, an extravert, was able to do so:

  I used to call introverted Bob "passive-aggressive" for keeping me waiting so long for a response while he looked around and ruminated about what he was thinking, as if I wasn't there. But I realized he wasn't trying to "get" me, so I would have him follow me into whatever activity I was doing while he considered and finally came out with a response. That worked well for both of us.

- Respect introverted friends' and family members' wishes if they prefer to be alone in times of stress or sadness. Anthony Starr notes, "In a culture in which interpersonal relationships are generally considered to provide the answer to every form of distress, it is sometimes difficult to persuade well-meaning helpers that solitude can be as therapeutic as emotional support."[1]

• When introverts opt for privacy, remember that this goes along with their inborn nature and is not necessarily a rejection of you. For example, Anthony Hopkins, an introverted actor, likes to socialize occasionally, but feels his main non-acting activities (playing the piano, composing music, and taking road trips) would be less pleasurable with other people along. "Most of the time," he told an interviewer, "I am enough."

> One's company, two's a crowd. —*Oscar Levant in the movie,* An American in Paris

• If you feel let down because your introvert isn't expressive enough, pay more attention to the words than their delivery. Extraverted Tamar multiplies her introverted partner's expressed emotions by ten; he divides hers by ten.

• Look for nonverbal signs of affection. Introverts are sometimes more comfortable expressing their feelings in writing or by their actions than through speaking.

• If your introverted friends or relatives go off to watch from the sidelines alone, don't assume they're unhappy:

> We extraverts belong to a club where we share the belief that interacting is always wonderful and fun. I'm sorry that introverts don't get to be part of this club. —*Nancy Kesselring*

• Invite introverts to join in, but don't push them:

> The leader of the meeting looked at the silent member and said, "You are quiet, but I think you have something to say." This introvert wouldn't have broken into the meeting to speak, for it would have seemed a disservice to her ideas to shout them out above the noise of the others. But since she was invited, she spoke—quietly and with great wisdom. —*Carolyn Rhodes*

• Question the adjectives and definitions you use for introverts: instead of "passive," perhaps they're "shy and gentle." Instead of "antisocial," perhaps "their main interests don't always involve other people." Instead of "self-centered" or "narcissistic," perhaps they have "satisfying inner lives."

• Let introverts know you appreciate them for being their own person:

> What makes a man interesting to me is when he's free. When he does not feel the need to look a certain way, to behave a certain way. When he's himself. Always. When he doesn't want to please everyone. —*Michele Laroque, actress*[2]

• In order to accept one another more easily, remember that neurological differences underlie introvert/extravert conflicts. Introverts have naturally busy minds, sometimes referred to as "inner wakefulness," and are easily overwhelmed by sensory stimuli. Extraverts become unpleasantly restless with too little stimulation, so they often seek action.

• Since our culture seems to be celebrating extraversion much of the time, extol the virtues of introversion as well.

Extraverts in Relationships

Extraverts like to do things together. The experiences themselves usually count more than pondering about them. If you're an extravert who feels you put out more than your share of energy, it helps to remember that introverts can also accomplish a lot, but their accomplishments will likely be of a different nature.

Knowing about type differences can be invaluable in preserving relationships. Extraverted Nancy, for instance, believes every occasion can be improved upon by adding more people. Her husband and son are both introverts, however. She might have labeled them as simply wrong, she told me, had she not understood type differences. Instead, she learned to respect their temperaments and they hers. Even though they're not crazy about social

activities themselves, they support her when she wants to invite friends over or throw a party.

Other traits to keep in mind: "Thinking type" extraverts can do with few compliments, but "feeling types" put effort into relating to others and depend on getting attention back. Extraverts are easier to "read" than introverts. Introverts aren't necessarily trying to keep a secret—disclosing their thoughts or feelings often just doesn't occur to them.

Solving Relationship Problems

Since we introverts can't always count on others to be sensitive to our needs, it's important that we become clear about the requirements of our temperament and try to create our own nurturing environment.

One Sunday morning last spring, I went outside to work in my garden, attracted by the stillness. In less than five minutes, an extraverted neighbor obliterated the peace and quiet by crawling under his car with his radio turned on full blast. (This is not meant to imply that all extraverts are insensitive.) Instead of going back into my house disappointed and disgruntled as I once might've done, I politely told him that I wanted to enjoy the quiet, not his music. He responded honestly and reasonably by explaining that he hated working on his car, but needed to fix it so he could attend a beach party. The radio made his job bearable. As we talked, it occurred to him that he could turn the volume down, put the radio closer to his ear, and we'd both be happy. "Great solution!" I said, relieved that he hadn't snarled, yelled, or called me a spoilsport for not wanting to hear his favorite radio station.

Conflicts between introverts and extraverts don't always end as successfully as this, but it's nice to know they can. After a conflict, a sincere apology is a positive way to extravert our feelings. It lets other people know we care about them. The introverted part includes mulling over what took place and trying to learn from it.

If you have trouble resolving conflict on your own, a well-trained, impartial therapist can help explain two people to each other and suggest ways to improve the relationship. John Weber, a therapist, says:

> With couples, I sometimes find that the more extraverted one quickly shoots from the hip and the other takes time to give consideration before answering. This is often a real bone of contention between them. I suggest that the introverted, contemplative one contract to give information within 24 hours and the extraverted, hip-shooter contract to respect this timing. It takes learning for both.

Besides introversion/extraversion, other personality differences that lead to misunderstandings include feeling vs. thinking, being down to earth vs. imaginative, and wanting closure vs. being open-minded. These differences are further discussed in Chapter 8. Another useful tool for dealing with different personalities is the Enneagram system, which helps people recognize their own gifts and limitations, as well as seeing the world from eight other perspectives.

RELATIONSHIP QUIZ

(Answer T for "true" and F for "false")

1. Introverts always feel relaxed on dates.
2. Introverts usually have more relationships than extraverts do.
3. Happiness for some introverts is being alone but with a memory of having recently been with others.
4. Relationships can't help anyone learn how to tolerate the ambiguities in life.
5. Most introverts like to use a minimum of words to express themselves, but some can't stop talking once they get started.
6. Some extraverts fear being left alone with nothing to do.

The way each of the nine Enneagram personalities interacts with each other in relationships is discussed in *Are You My Type, Am I Yours?*, a book I wrote with Renee Baron. The nine personal-

7. One reason to develop both introversion and extraversion is for flexibility in case an important part of your life stops working. For example: a relationship ends, the children leave home, you lose your job or become injured.

8. Often, introverts go over issues in their heads and come to conclusions alone, while extraverts figure out what they think by talking it out.

9. Extraverts are often more aware than introverts of the intersubjectivity of relating.

10. One reason introverts tend to be loyal after investing in a relationship is that it's hard to lose it and have to make another connection.

11. Introverts have a great capacity for happiness in an individualistic way; they are sometimes less happy in the social arena.

ANSWERS:
1. false; 2. false; 3. true; 4. false; 5. true; 6. true; 7. true; 8. true; 9. false; 10. true; 11. true

Words by Nigel Thompson

ities are the Romantic, the Observer (these two are the most introverted types), the Perfectionist, the Helper, the Achiever, the Questioner, the Adventurer, the Boss, and the Peacemaker.

Appreciating Each Other

It is our humanness and our own brand
of it that we must come to love.
—John Weber

One of the gifts I admire most in extraverts is their ability to express gusto and inspire enthusiasm. Some extraverts know how to readily put people at ease by choosing just the right words. We introverts, however, often need time to ponder how sincere we feel before we're willing to speak. By the time we've prepared ourselves, the window of opportunity may have passed.

I'm impressed with the ability of many extraverts to be tactful *spontaneously* and I would like to emulate it. But in the end, I satisfy myself with the knowledge that we introverts can do well in other areas that might not demand such quickness, such as pursuing subjects in depth, being good listeners, and silently holding someone's hand when that's what is needed.

Just as introverts sometimes surprise everyone by popping up with an extraverted side nobody knew about, extraverts often keep an introverted part of themselves hidden. I knew Valerie for several decades before I discovered the poet in her. She thought of herself as someone who was important for getting things done in the world, however, and didn't take me seriously when I expressed an interest in her writing. Finally, a serious illness forced her to slow down and she devoted some attention to her inner life. After that, she was happy to share some of her writings with me.

3

Parenting and Teaching Children

We need to love our children for who they are,
not how outgoing we want them to be.
—*Dr. Carducci*

A young mother and her two well-behaved sons, around four and five years old, sat down across from me on the subway. The younger, more serious and self-contained brother had found a feather and was examining it from every angle. Then he exchanged it for his plastic superhero doll and slowly moved its arms into different positions. In the 20 minutes that I watched him, he never moved his eyes away from what he was doing. His involvement in his own world is typical of an introvert. The older, apparently extraverted brother flirted with everyone around him. Always active and busy, he looked at me at least 20 times to see how I was reacting to him. Fortunately, the boys' mother seemed comfortable with both styles of behavior.

Most quiet or inward children are probably born with a naturally introverted temperament. There can be other reasons for children having relatively withdrawn behavior, however, usually stemming from their early years. These include having delicate health, living in an isolated place, and moving often.

Understanding introversion and extraversion helps parents and teachers perceive their children's actions and attitudes and give them the appropriate support. A gregarious, take-charge, extraverted child, for example, needs to be treated differently from a sensitive, individualistic introvert.

Introverted Children

Introverted children usually feel good about the part of their lives where they are self-sufficient and able to explore, probe, and experience the joy of putting things together. If they sense the main adults in their lives want them to be different from the way they are, however, they are apt to feel inferior or depressed. I wasn't directly criticized for not being more sociable, but I could tell how much other children and adults around me valued the trait of being outgoing. Why, for example, was I uncomfortable meeting new people? I'd be happy alone, but I didn't know how to make a place for myself when I attempted to enter in at school recesses. Eventually, I'd climb down to the meadow at the edge of the school grounds to play contentedly by myself. When the bell rang and I returned to class, I always wondered what, if anything, my classmates thought of me for not joining them in their games.

Introverted Carl Jung entered in with the other children, but had the feeling he was betraying himself in doing so:

> I found my schoolmates alienated me from myself. When I was with them, I became different from the way I was at home. It seemed to me that the change in myself was due to the influence of my school fellows, which somehow misled me or compelled me to be different from what I thought I was. The influence of this wider world seemed to me dubious if not altogether suspect and, in some obscure way, hostile. [1]

Their Behavior

Getting along well in groups requires the ability to adjust to quick changes and to handle busy and noisy environments. Introverted

children usually have nervous systems that do best in gentle and quiet surroundings.

When I was a child, I became sick from listening to Mrs. Fowler's singing voice. The two poles of her vibrato would wobble farther and farther apart as her loud and grating voice soared uncontrollably above the others. One Sunday during hymns, when I was about eight, I thought I'd have a nervous breakdown if I had to listen to this clashing noise for one more minute.

Some introverted children are shy or fearful. When this is extreme, they might be so frightened of people they suffer from "social anxiety" or "social phobia." This means they are so nervous, or attached to their parents, they are afraid to speak, as though something horrible would happen to them if they did. These  children often refuse to go to school or avoid birthday parties and sleepovers. Doctors sometimes prescribe drugs to raise the level of serotonin in their brains.

Shame is a sense that one is outside the social group or doesn't belong as a whole person. How different would it be for

introverts if people said, "Ah, they are the ones that go inside and find truths for the people. How they move among us, seeing things and bringing unity. Their inner energy is a beautiful power." —*John Weber*

Shame, a combination of guilt and depression, stems from a sense of not being respected for who one is. If parents of small children express disgust instead of the love they have come to expect, the introverts will usually withdraw and hide, while the extraverts will often respond by trying all the harder to win approval or by acting out.

Children need to be shown they are loved at the deepest level. When they don't behave in a way that matches the image their parents have in their mind, their parents are likely to treat them like outsiders and show disdain. Parents and teachers must watch out for this with introverted children especially. Kids can even experience neutrality as rejection. I wished that all of a sudden I would no longer be quiet, shy, and frightened but would feel relaxed around people. To remember what seemed like a constant family refrain of "why are you so quiet, what are you always so afraid of?" is really distressing. I always thought that being an extravert was the ideal and that being "quiet, shy, reserved, private, and fearful" was bad because those were my family's values. Finding out that these behaviors and feelings were normal was an enormous surprise to me. — *Joan Rosenberg Ryan, an introvert*

Extraverted Children

Extraverted children encounter fewer stumbling blocks than introverts when it comes to venturing out and interacting with people. They often take pleasure in finding out the answers to "how do I fit in?" and "how can I impact that?" by taking action and learning from the feedback. Solitude is a different route to self-discovery, but one that extraverts tend to find boring.

It is only when children have experienced a contented, relaxed sense of being alone with, and then without, the mother that they are able to discover what they really need or want, irrespective of what others may expect or try to foist upon them. The capacity to be alone thus becomes linked with self-discovery and self-realization; with becoming aware of one's deepest needs, feelings, and impulses. —*Anthony Storr*[2]

Extraverted children tend to be busy, optimistic, and confident, to seek attention, and to organize games and other activities. At times they sense others are perceiving them as too bouncy, wild, and overwhelming, however. If their high level of energy is not met, they can feel neglected.

Their Behavior

Introverted children aren't the only ones to suffer from anxiety. For example, active, go-explore, extraverted children can become nervous wrecks if their parents always worry about the environment being dangerous. This will affect a quiet, absorbing, introverted child less.

If one's behavior is honored, it does not sour.
I can think of extraverts who are deeply ashamed.
They too are outsiders but their behavior may cloak this.
Sometimes the denial of self is great enough for anger
to surface in physical symptoms or destructive behavior.
—John Weber, an extravert

Robert's extremely introverted mother was uncomfortable having an extraverted child. She didn't appreciate his exuberance—in fact, it frightened her. As a result, he kept his true personality muffled, sat on his anger, and developed a terrible rash that required his face be bandaged. If Robert's  mother had been educated in personality type, she probably would have handled their differences in a more constructive way.

Siblings

Personalities of siblings sometimes push one another in opposite directions. In my family, my older sister expressed an interest in

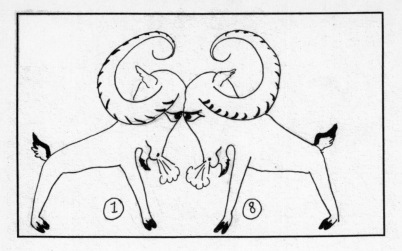

science; I liked art and music. She preferred purple; I preferred blue. She was talkative; I was quiet. After researching this book, I wondered: Would I have been less introverted if I had been born first?

According to Frank J. Sulloway's book, *Born to Rebel*[3], *oldest children* tend to identify with the power and authority of their parents. If they are near the midline of introversion/extraversion by nature, being born first may tilt them toward extraversion. First-borns are likely to be ambitious, assertive, self-confident, jealous, punitive, concerned about their status, and politically conservative. Since *later-born* children need to make their own way, they tend to be independent, imaginative, unconventional, challenging, and introverted. If they are extraverted, they can be especially rebellious or radical. Since *middle children* often grow up having the least personal power, they tend to get along by being flexible and compromising. Parent-child conflicts can change these patterns.

As for twins, I first saw fraternal twins Ania and Kim across the street when they were two or three weeks old. Ania appeared introverted (within herself), while Kim seemed extraverted (more attentive to what was going on around her). Now they are 14. Ania still tends toward introversion and Kim still tends toward extraversion, supporting the argument in favor of nature over nurture. Their father wholeheartedly believes in the revelation that his daughters were born who they are, and considers it one of the gifts of having twins.

Parenting Tips

In order for parents and teachers to observe children accurately, I recommend they learn about the other six personality preferences measured on the Myers-Briggs test besides introversion and extraversion: *sensing, intuition, feeling, thinking, perceiving,* and *judging* (see Chapter 8). I also suggest they study the nine Enneagram personality types to help understand different kinds of children, learning styles, and the dynamics between their personality styles and their children's.

The nine Enneagram types are the *Perfectionist,* the *Helper,* the *Achiever,* the *Romantic,* the *Observer,* the *Questioner,* the *Adventurer,* the *Boss,* and the *Peacemaker.* Most Observers and Romantics are introverted; most Adventurers and Achievers are extraverted.

Here's an example of how learning about personality types can ease the parenting process. Quentin, whose parents were at

Tips on parenting both types

MBTI

As a musician, I'm always asking people to come into my world. With (my) kids you can't do that. You have to go into their world.
- Bruce Springsteen.

Enneagram

Achiever   Romantic   Boss   Helper

Four of the nine Enneagram types

war about how to raise him, was a fearful *Questioner* in the Enneagram system. Unfortunately, his mother, an unhealthy version of a *Helper,* had a deep yearning for human connection and learned she could use his fear to insure his dependency on her. This only instilled more doubt and anxiety in him. His father, also a *Questioner,* wanted to help Quentin feel safe by encouraging confidence and trust. By studying the Enneagram, Quentin's mother became aware of her own need to be needed and saw what this was doing to their son. She also saw how important it was to empower their son rather than overprotect him, so she joined her husband in helping Quentin overcome his fears.

In general, parents should allow their children to seek out their own path, whether it be toward introversion or toward extraversion. Here are a few tips to help you help them:

- Alter your usual activities, if necessary, to present a mixture of introversion and extraversion for your children to model. Bob found himself going to the ballet for the first time in order to take his kids. Tom was never crazy about sports, but he gladly watched his kids play baseball. Joyce demanded total privacy in her painting studio, but her one exception was to let her son fingerpaint alongside her.

- Set an example by being involved in your own challenging interests. Tell your children which activities you might want to take up in the future, show them where you work, and let them see that your own friendships are important to you.
- Practice speaking to your children in a direct way. Maria von Franz says, ". . . Sugary hypocrisy, faint praise, loud uncertainty, cruel correction does more damage than the direct expression of negative feelings: anger, dislike, panic, etc."
- Parents' personalities can cause stress on a child. Beware of too much correcting or advice-giving, living off of or resenting the attention given your children, providing too little

guidance, being too busy to spend time with your kids, and fretting, warning, cautioning, or bossing them too much.

- Be patient when teaching your children to do chores. If they don't follow instructions right away, sometimes parents get impatient and do the task themselves, which instills a sense of shame.

- Classes for children who are shunned, ignored, or teased on the playground may interest you. Among other things, child psychologists and speech therapists teach "how to greet each other, how to introduce kids to other kids, and where to go after you say hello":

> . . . [In these classes, kids learn how to] get along with their peers by being paired with children who are having similar difficulties. . . . During weekly, hour-long sessions, children as young as 4 and as old as 14 learn everything from how to start a conversation to how to handle teasing.
>
> [These children's] style of play is so introverted or so extraverted that they either aren't making friends at all or their over-the-top behavior turns friends off. They don't know when they're standing too close to someone or too far away. They don't know when their voice is too loud or too low. They don't make eye contact or they run right over someone in conversation. They overpower or they cower. It's not just learning what to do, therapists say. It's practicing it over and over in different settings. —*Diana Walsh*[4]

Parenting Introverted Children

The key to parenting introverted children is to help them feel protected but not overprotected. This requires monitoring them while being mindful to not be intrusive. Let them know you're nearby and available.

- Encourage independence to give your child a firm base to jump off from, the safety to be seen, and the grounding to interact spontaneously.

• Keep in mind that introverted children often study or practice better when no one is watching them. For example, Thelonius Monk, the great introverted be-bop pianist, once took offense that Count Basie had been watching him play—and threatened to retaliate by watching Basie back. In introverted Patrick's case, he became an excellent artist not from taking art classes, but from studying library books. As introvert Nigel Thompson puts it:

> I've always learned best when alone. My dad tried to teach me to ride a bike when I was five or six. He kept trying and trying until he finally gave up. Then he saw me go into the garage for a while and next thing he knew I was riding my bike out of the garage. I just can't concentrate on what I'm doing as well when I'm concentrating on someone else.

• Consider partitioning off a pleasing private space for your introverted child, possibly with sheets or scarves.

• Expose your child to other children who might become appropriate friends. Since introverts often march to their own drummer, it may take extra effort to find peers with similar interests and ways of looking at life.

• Be aware of how your relationship with one of your children may affect your other children, especially sensitive ones. For example, Cathy used to listen behind closed doors, terrified, as her older sister and mother hurled anger at each other. Believing she would not survive a similar encounter herself, she became overly conciliatory by doing everything in her power to avoid arguments.

Teaching Tips

At school, extraverts tend to come up with answers to teachers' questions quickly and find it difficult to wait for their turn to speak. They often do well academically up to age 12 or 15, when social motivation is of prime importance. Introverts tend to excel in later grades due to perseverance, self-discipline, and their ability to study independently.

• Offer children a balanced mixture of introverted and extraverted activities, providing for periods of privacy as well as togetherness. Playing an instrument, for example, can be done either alone or in groups.

• For those who have trouble entering class discussions, it helps for the teacher to say, "Is there anything anyone wants to add before we say goodbye?" Quiet students can let out what they may have been sitting on and the others can get a chance to hear what they've been thinking.

• For certain *sensate* types, school is especially difficult. Practical, hands-on teaching helps. Augie Wagele, a sensate type and a 7-Adventurer in the Enneagram system, states:

> My own company is fine, but I also like doing activities with friends. I feel really frustrated, though, if someone else is controlling my space or pace. I don't do well with school. If I really want to learn something, I'm all ears. But if I don't, there's no way I can pay attention. When people around me are stressed out, I want to go be by myself. Challenges interest me—seeing how things work, trying to fix things that are broken, and bringing humor to a situation. I also like remembering things about people that I can surprise them with later, like the model of car they drive.

• Give children enough time to experiment and be creative. Bjork, the famous Icelandic singer and songwriter, complained that in music school her teachers only wanted to "fill the students up from the outside" instead of encouraging them to express what's inside.[5]

• A child who is allowed to follow her bliss will explore what she is interested in, and learn to handle more and more complexity. When I was a child, I loved music above all else. I fell in love with a recording of Rimsky-Korsakov's *Sheherazade* and painstakingly figured out how to play it on the piano. I gradually taught myself more and more. When I needed help learning to read music, I begged my parents to give me piano lessons.

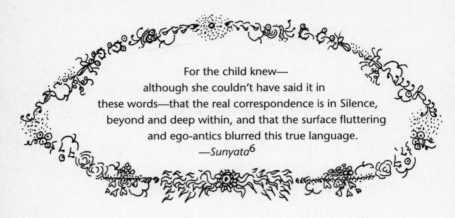

For the child knew—
although she couldn't have said it in
these words—that the real correspondence is in Silence,
beyond and deep within, and that the surface fluttering
and ego-antics blurred this true language.
—*Sunyata*[6]

- Introverts often can't relax unless they are alone with the teacher or in a very small class. If large classes are unavoidable, try to meet their needs by creating enclosed spaces within the classroom or making use of the school library.

- When introverted children have recreational time, allow them to go to the library or another room where they can comfortably read or play board games. Otherwise, the introverts may find themselves on the playground with nothing to do.

- Introverted children often appear slower because they have more going on internally. Avoid measuring children by their verbal-response speed. Harry Gans, an introvert, recalls, "I remember the time in elementary school when my mother and teacher met on Parent's Day. The teacher told mom that I was slower than the other students, but my answers were usually right."

- Be aware that introverted children sometimes misbehave in order to be put in isolation. This can be a sign that a situation is overly stimulating (i.e., too noisy or busy) for introverts and is causing too much stress. See what happens if you create a calmer, quieter atmosphere for the child.

QUIZ ABOUT CHILDREN

(Answer T for "true" and F for "false")

1. Under the age of ten, introverts always feel comfortable in social situations.
2. Shyness often includes a painful feeling that the whole room is staring at you, even if it's not.
3. Western societies never press introverted children to go in a direction they don't want to go in.
4. Many introverts tend to be thin-skinned.
5. Introversion/depression/phobias are related, while extraversion/mania/hysteria are related.
6. Children thrive when they feel perceived.
7. Introverted children often do well when gently invited to join in. If they refuse, it's best not to pressure them but to leave the door open in case they change their minds.

ANSWERS:
1. false; 2. true; 3. false; 4. true; 5. true; 6. true; 7. true

• In our extraverted world, children are exposed to many examples of achievers and heroes. Celebrate introversion as well by teaching children about the virtues of working on something in depth, finding out how things work, silence, and listening. Says Nigel Thompson, an introvert:

> For all the people who expound on this and that and push for changing this and controlling that, it is necessary to have others who just sit peacefully with things in quiet consciousness and awareness. This is just as important as all the big noise. On the silent Earth, things come and go, the Earth keeps turning. No one usually pays much attention to it, but if it decides to change everyone will notice. I'm thinking of the wars going on right now in the world. Eventually, the survivors will need people who just sit with them, hear their stories, and understand them. Give them a peaceful Earth, a space within which to heal.

4

About Adolescents

Adolescence as we've come to know it is a modern phenome-
non. In previous societies and tribal cultures, the adult usually
merges quickly out of childhood through participation in
puberty rites. Now, however, for ten years or more, modern
adolescents must make attempts to say farewell to childhood
without the benefit of such socially sanctioned rites of passage.
—*D. Gentry*[1]

Adolescents are often involved in their own projects or social
activities and may be absent from home a lot or otherwise inac-
cessible. Thus giving special attention to nurturing their self-
esteem and well-being can be especially challenging for their
parents. At this age, however, both introverts and extraverts experience more upheavals, disorder, and contradictions than at
any other time in life.

If I was ever at all interested in becoming a teacher, I decided
against it once and for all when I saw what a hard time my teach-

ers had trying to control some of my fellow adolescents. Certain 14- to 15-year-old boys, especially, tested every boundary they could think of. Unless the teacher ruled with an iron hand, the classroom atmosphere could dissolve into utter chaos. On the other side of adolescence, children of that age can also bring incredible freshness and joy to a home. I enjoyed the ways my kids and their friends could express affection for one another at this age and the enthusiasm with which they explored life.

Introverted Adolescents

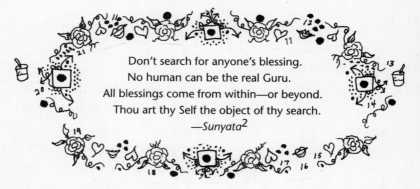

Don't search for anyone's blessing.
No human can be the real Guru.
All blessings come from within—or beyond.
Thou art thy Self the object of thy search.
—*Sunyata*[2]

The introverted side of adolescence (for both introverts and extraverts) is expressed as isolation, idealism, inspiration, wondering, dreaming, inner chaos, and pondering the purpose of life and what it means to be human. Introverts sometimes wish they had a road map to follow to help them solve their problems and find their own voices. They may feel unseen unless they are computer whizzes or excel at sports or music. If they are quiet, their peers may project onto them that they are snobbish, boring, or even sneaky. If they are talkative, they may wonder if they talk too much.

Some introverted adolescents find fulfillment in their interests and close friends, but avoid social occasions such as parties and dances because they find them superficial and boring or scary and painful. Of the introverts who *do* attend these functions, some enjoy them, some go even though they feel miserable and out of place, and some have mixed experiences.

• Felix was good at science and sports and could play the piano with ease, but most social interactions felt unnatural unless he knew someone well. He studied hard, did well in all subjects, participated in class discussions, was active in the literary club, and spent his noon hours in the library reading and helping arrange books. His social life improved greatly when his adolescence was over.

• Who else but an introvert would live alone two miles from the nearest paved road? If you had known Steve in his adolescence, however, you might have pegged him as an outgoing, talkative, and confident extravert. His apparent extraversion was the result of extreme modeling and pressure by his family. It took three decades for him to settle into his true, introverted nature.

• Madonna, a 14-year-old introvert, alternates between feeling attractive, which she is, and wondering when someone will de-

cide to tell her how strange she is. When with her peers, she often feels too exposed, but she almost always feels satisfied when she's alone doing her creative projects.

• The teenage group at the church I belonged to happened to be made up mainly of introverts. We knew we were different from most other kids, though I don't know if we knew why, and we felt lucky to have found each other. It is still important for me to have some good introverted friends I can talk to. I also have some valuable extraverted friends.

Schools should have clubs for introverts.

Extraverted Adolescents

The extraverted side of adolescence, for both introverts and extraverts, includes stubbornness, aggression, seeking relationships and role models, an appetite for new kinds of excitement, and surges of independence. Extraverted adolescents' paths may be clearer than introverts'. They are more likely to either copy adults, follow society's rules, or go against them. Extraverted adolescents keep moving and like joining in.

• Jose was not challenged enough at school or at home so he joined a gang for the excitement. His parents might've been able to steer him in another direction, such as competitive sports, but it didn't occur to them how seriously he needed more outlets for his energy until it was too late.

• Sixteen-year-old Harriet's decisions were driven by a voice that said, "If this is what people are doing, you should do it, too!" One day, this extravert found herself stranded on a desert island. With time on her hands, she discovered who she was independently from other people. When she returned home, she surprised everyone by following her *own* desires.

• Extraverted Knute was class and student body president. He expressed his many facets by an ever-changing persona. Arriving at school early and leaving late, he squeezed in almost every club and activity. He was good all day, but when night came he rebelled by drinking and tearing around in his car.

You know you're an extravert if you think "bored to death" is redundant.

Introversion/extraversion is largely inborn, but how others react to a person's temperament depends on the culture. If introverts made up 70 to 75 percent of the U.S. population instead of 25 to 30 percent, your child's social life, especially, would be quite different.

How Introverts and Extraverts Differ Neurologically

It can be helpful to parents, teachers, and adolescents themselves to look at aspects of adolescence in an objective way. Here are some central nervous system differences between introverts and

extraverts that scientists have documented (also see Chapter 7 for more information on this subject):

- Introverts can concentrate longer than extraverts on a video display where there is little stimulation.
- Extraverts' verbal ability improves with a combination of time pressure and ingestion of caffeine. Introverts' performances decline with the same combination.
- Extraverts tolerate relatively high levels of noise and pain.
- Introverts can tolerate longer periods of sensory deprivation.
- Extraverts pay less attention than introverts to internal stimuli that inhibit behavior.
- Extraverts perform better on tasks that require gross motor action than on tasks that require motor control or inhibition.

This has not been proven, but some scientists believe the impulsive, erratic, rebellious behavior of teenagers that is often blamed on hormones may be related to shifts at puberty in the part of the brain that regulates reasoning and planning.[3]

Adolescents and Relationships

Relationships and longing in adolescence have both introverted and extraverted implications, can challenge the child's sense of identity, and can arouse emotions from euphoria to despair.

Take childhood buddies Tyler and Ivan, who dealt with similar experiences in very different manners. Extraverted Tyler charged confidently into new social situations, while his introverted friend since kindergarten, Ivan, held back. When the boys were 16, a friend of theirs, Oscar, who had been seeing how far he could go with people lately, marched up to Tyler, folded his arms diffidently, and told him he didn't like him. Leaning casually against the wall, Tyler looked a bit amused and said, "Does that mean we won't be playing baseball on Friday?" Then he went home, got involved in a game of ping-pong, and forgot all about the encounter.

Later that day, Oscar marched up to introverted Ivan, folded his arms, and told Ivan he didn't like him. Ivan was flustered and didn't know what to do, and he heard himself blurt out, in a voice he didn't recognize, that he had never liked Oscar either. It wasn't even true. It was several years before Ivan stopped second-guessing himself about the incident: "Could I have handled it better? Maybe I should have punched him. I wish I hadn't said anything," and so on.

Twenty years later, Tyler and Ivan were still reacting in the same way. Tyler tended to look to the next activity he could engage in and not look back all that much at small choices he had made that day, while introverted Ivan kept a detailed journal, including word for word conversations he had had.

Fu-Ting, the extraverted teenager, is an officer in the student government, belongs to several after-school clubs, and likes to watch TV shows with her friends. She reads books that sell well, figuring that if others like them she'll probably like them, too—

plus there will be plenty of people to discuss them with. Fu-Ting doesn't understand why her introverted brother, Yo-Yo, keeps to himself so much or why he reads and rereads books nobody else has heard of. Yo-Yo, on the other hand, criticizes Fu-Ting for floating along on the surface of her "frenzied and scattered" life. Instead of appreciating their differences, Fu-Ting and Yo-Yo look down upon one another for having the "wrong" values.

Developing a Persona

"Persona" is the part of personality that me-
diates between ego (who you know yourself to be) and the outside world. It
includes roles you play or masks you
wear in different circumstances.

Some adolescents adopt a shock-
ing persona, which may or may not
conform to their peers, to help them

break away from their parents. Shy or
withdrawn adolescents may feel
they don't have a persona or that
their persona is "out of order."
Extreme extraverts may become so attached to playing a
role, they deny themselves
the chance of making their
own order out of the inner
chaos of adolescence.

The task of adolescents is
to begin forging lives for themselves, but gaining enough independence to discern who *they* are
can be tricky. Some find it easier to
distance themselves from their parents
by wastefully throwing out everything about
them. The best way to head this off is to encourage your children
early on to question their beliefs, search for meaning and authen-
ticity within themselves, and form their own opinions.

Introverted adolescents ask, "How can I be myself and get
people to relate to my private world?" "Where are my models?"
Most introverts have a good sense of who they are, but since
they are so different from extraverts, and even from one introvert
to the next, they often have trouble knowing who they are in
other people's eyes. If they have put something out they have
created, only to have it denigrated, their vulnerable connection
with the world becomes even more endangered. Introverted adolescents need gentle encouragement to learn more about themselves, use their talents, and find like-minded friends to help
solidify their place in the world and make a constructive transition to adulthood.

Text continued on page 82.

SELF-ESTEEM QUIZ

You must know adolescents who can't bear to think they aren't perfect. Self-esteem can be damaged by neglect, abuse, too much criticism, or poor sibling relationships. Problems such as these can be eased by children improving their self-esteem. If they are introverts, they will learn to act on their feelings and ideas. If they are extraverts, they will learn to think before they act. High self-esteem goes hand in hand with versatility, feeling helpful, the ability to be assertive, accepting one's imperfections, and making self-improvements.

"Genuine self-esteem is achieved when we feel competent and successful in the areas of our life that are important to us." —*Bonnie J. Golden*

Either check the items that apply to your adolescent (to the best of your knowledge) or ask the adolescent to check the items that apply. You both might want to take the quiz and compare your answers.

Group I. I like myself especially when:
1. I feel strong and enthusiastic and am not just faking it.
2. I feel safe enough to feel and express my own thoughts and feelings.
3. I'm developing a skill—music, computers, athletics, science, etc.
4. I'm involved in a discussion with a friend who thinks for herself or himself.
5. I'm working on a project I really like.
6. I'm taking a walk or observing people or nature.
7. I'm reading or I'm learning from hands-on experiences.
8. I'm earning my own money.
9. I'm teaching someone something I'm good at.
10. I'm comfortable in my home, whether with my family or alone.
11. I have an interesting e-mail correspondence with a good friend.

12. I'm feeling useful.

13. Others see me for who I am.

14. I can put my practical or creative abilities to good use.

Group II. I like myself especially when:

1. I'm speaking up forcefully.

2. People call on me for my leadership.

3. I'm the life of the party.

4. Most of the people are on my side.

5. I set important goals for myself and meet them.

6. I can change people's moods.

7. I'm seen as confident and knowledgeable.

8. I feel attractive and well dressed.

9. I'm acknowledged for my athletic ability.

10. I'm praised for scholastic achievements.

11. I'm elected to student offices.

12. I'm out and about accomplishing things.

13. I'm straightforward and open about myself.

14. I'm competing.

Introverted adolescents are more likely to check items in Group I. Extraverted adolescents are more likely to check items in Group II.

Parenting Tips

Many parents want their adolescents to have lots of friends, like parties, and feel comfortable with people. If your children don't fit this extraverted mold, however, they are not necessarily any less happy, fulfilled, or able to contribute to the world. Expressing acceptance of your children will help them find out who they are, show how they feel inside on the outside when they want to, gain confidence, and form their own adult personalities.

Balancing introversion and extraversion.

• Encourage your children to connect with happy, sad, fearful, and romantic parts of themselves through music, books, and movies, and to become acquainted with peers who have similar tastes and interests.

• Help your children explore new interests. One of these may form the basis for a lifelong passion or career.

• Engage with your children in imagining creative possibilities for their future that reflect their identity.

QUIZ ON ADOLESCENTS AND INTROVERSION/EXTRAVERSION

(Answer T for "true" and F for "false")

1. Raising teenagers is like nailing Jell-O to a tree . . .
2. . . . so no amount of learning on the part of parents and teachers helps.
3. While introverts and extraverts can both excel in most areas, extraverts are naturally more attracted to prestige or power in social situations.
4. It is not unusual for adolescents to identify themselves as extraverts, even if they are introverts.
5. Sometimes temperamentally introverted adolescents have typically extraverted values and temperamentally extraverted adolescents have typically introverted values.
6. Introverted adolescents thrive in large groups, especially when they are put on the spot and asked "embarrassing" questions.
7. Books praising introversion help non-extraverted adolescents learn to honor and respect themselves. This is important in our society, where many of the prevailing values are those of the extraverted majority.
8. An attitude that is not constructive in dealing with introverted adolescents is: "There's nothing wrong with you that changing into an extravert won't fix."

ANSWERS:
1. true; 2. false; 3. true; 4. true; 5. true; 6. false; 7. true; 8. true

• If your child is extraverted, encourage the ability to be alone. Some may not immediately see the point of solitude, but there come times in everyone's life where it's necessary to slow down or be alone for a while.

• Be a good example by showing your kids you value quiet and private time yourself.

• Try to see your children's points of view. Discuss with them ways you are the same and different from them. Let them know you want them to learn how to stand on their own two feet *and* you want to be sure they are safe.

• Encourage your children to develop competencies in several areas of life.

• Teach your introverted adolescents to communicate their need for quiet, the reason it sometimes take them longer to respond, their preference for small groups (if these apply), or anything else that might help them feel more at ease when they are with people.

• Be careful not to automatically blame your kids' peer groups if your adolescents suddenly seem unfamiliar to you. This isn't meant to imply that there aren't legitimate reasons for concern at times.

• Be sensitive when an adolescent tries on a new role.

As parents, therapists, and educators, we have to contend with our own cruel streak that wants to insult, scorn, mock, or shame a developing persona. Perhaps this irrational urge can be traced back to having been shamed ourselves as adolescents when trying out a new role . . . Or our scorn may have the same primal source as the cruel delight adolescents take in mocking an adult persona. Whatever the reason, adolescents assuming a new persona are extremely vulnerable, and out of respect for the process, we must watch this impulse in ourselves and try to tread lightly.—*Richard Frankel*[4]

While some parents mess up their children's lives miserably, even those who have raised their children with the epitome of love and understanding are sometimes wrongly accused:

Later, Bosco stopped blaming all of his problems on his childhood.

5
Creativity

Creativity, to me, means bringing new perspectives to old
ideas, finding connections with things that at first glance don't
seem to have any, and playing with life and situations with
freshness and delight.
—*Mary Porter-Chase*

This chapter focuses on how we as individuals benefit from our
own creativity. Every time we engage in the creative process, our
inner lives are reflected back to us and we see ourselves a little differently. For example, if we draw a picture of a dream we had last
night, not only must we translate the dream to graphic form, we are
also making choices about where to place the objects on the paper,

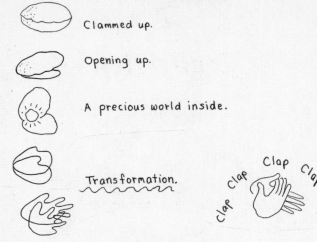

Acclamation

Clammed up.

Opening up.

A precious world inside.

Transformation.

Clap Clap Clap Clap Clap Clap

the colors to use, and so on. No matter what our artistic skill is, we are experiencing the psyche of a human being we didn't entirely know before. We are learning something new about ourselves.

Some ignore their inner lives. Some share them easily. Others feel ambivalent about whether to express themselves or keep their inner thoughts and feelings hidden away—they may long to share them but fear they can't be transported to the outside world. What's important is to engage in a creative project and to applaud yourself for expressing yourself in a new way.

> I think the whole purpose of creation is to unshackle
> oneself, to be free, to find out what you are . . .
> Without this self-questioning and self-refinement,
> there is no process of elevation possible.
> —Robert Engman, sculptor[1]

The Creative Process

The creative process is the means by which we find and express our unique voice. It involves focusing our awareness and abilities on that which is most meaningful to us at the time. Creativity can be motivated by curiosity, the need to solve or transcend a problem, the desire to communicate or grow, and it can be inexplicable. Following are four of the ways we create:

THE INTROVERTED PROCESS   The introverted process takes place in the psyche beyond the reach of conscious knowing, resulting in fresh ways of seeing, feeling, and thinking. Out of this, practical, innovative, or imaginative new directions may emerge. Some feel they help the introverted process along by turning their backs on the world and finding stillness.

> *In the plant kingdom there are fallow times*
> *But roots spread underground,*
> *Blossoms will appear in the spring,*
> *What is missing will be found.*

THE EXTRAVERTED PROCESS   The line between introverted and extraverted processing is not a clear one. Extraverted processing involves more action: reacting in response to others, creating jointly, or living in a new way. Both introverts and extraverts use both introverted and extraverted processing.

FLOW   The state called "flow" is a certain kind of creative process. When it happens, you feel your thoughts and actions are being directed by something outside of yourself, as if from a far-off place. At the same time, you feel closer to the center of who you are.

According to George Nelson, an industrial designer,

> You disengage the motor and get into a mood of no thought, sort of an empty, relaxed, or detached mood . . . You turn off your conscious mind with all its buzzing and scurrying, and just coast . . . You have ideas while shaving, but what you're doing while shaving is sort of disengaging because you're concentrating on this semi-automatic act. It is my experience that unless you turn off the active conscious mind, this idea quite possibly won't arrive.[2]

Writer Isaac Bashevis Singer believes that "in some cases, you have a feeling as if some little imp or devil is standing behind you and dictating to you, but he gives it to you slowly, drop by drop."[3]

Mihaly Csikszentmihaly, a psychologist, notes:

> The human body is capable of hundreds of separate functions—seeing, hearing, touching, running, swimming, throwing, catching, climbing up mountains and climbing down caves, to name only a few—and to each of these there correspond flow experiences . . . The simple act of moving the body across space becomes a source of complex feedback that provides optimal experience and adds strength to the self. Each sensory organ, each motor function can be harnessed to the production of flow.[4]

INSTANT CREATIVITY   Sam's songs burst forth full-blown—it's just a matter of writing them down. "They come to me involuntarily, in my sleep!" he said. "If I don't get up and sing the song into my recorder right away, I become physically ill." The other areas of his musical life, practicing with his band, sound mixing, and arranging events, however, involve intentional hard work.

How We Profit from Being Creative

"'Depth' is an odd word," Isaiah Berlin said.
"It's a metaphor, but you can't translate it into other terms.
Depth means penetrating into something very basic in oneself,
and touching it, and feeling an electric shock."
—A. Alvarez[5]

For centuries, sages have been advising: "Know yourself." When we create, we get to see previously hidden parts of ourselves. We learn who we are by observing the choices we made, the stories we invented, and the symbols we used. It's a bonus when other people benefit from what we have created by learning to see things in a new way.

Marcel Proust once wrote, "The writer's work is merely a kind of optical instrument that makes it possible for the reader to discern what, without this book, he would perhaps never have seen in himself."

Jung believed that each person's primary task is to integrate the ego with the unconscious or shadow personality. When we draw our dreams, for example, we see images that go against our conscious attitudes, so we come face to face with our *other* side.

Creating—by exploring who we are, learning new things, and staying focused—is a healthy and positive way to spend time. Being consumed creatively feels like playing did when we were small. For some, it *is* playing. We are not free to play or create, however, if we impose a time limit on it, use it to impress someone, or think it should be done in a certain way.

THOU SHALT NOT SHOULD ON THYSELF!

The Creative Spark

We are grateful for those creative geniuses whose work has changed our lives for the better.

The creative spark takes place at the point where introversion and extraversion meet. Both introverts and extraverts gather information from outside themselves and process it together with information stored inside, resulting in new combinations and patterns.

The introverted process consists of going toward our center to find new awareness and meaning. The extraverted process is the journey of returning to conscious life and manifesting our findings in the world.

In the first half of life, we learn what we're good at doing and how to relate to others. In midlife, around our forties, we go through a transformation (similar in ways to adolescence) and become aware of aspects of ourselves we've neglected. The second half of life can stimulate creativity: introverts often become more interested in putting their work out in the world for others to see; extraverts often apply their energy to quieter, more solitary activities. In the second half of life, the ideal is to strengthen our weak-

est psychological functions and become more whole. Jung called this "individuation." This doesn't always happen, however.

The Role of the Unconscious

> Jung accepted with absolute directedness and seriousness
> the reality and importance of the unconscious and its
> contents as an essential part of the whole personality.
> —*June Singer*

In daily life, we fear that Freudian slips and other signs from our unconscious might threaten our ego and jeopardize our relationships. Dreams, however, are tucked in safely beyond the reach of

The Mystery of the Interior

our ego-needs and others' needs, and are valuable for giving us a glimpse into the unconscious. We may run into frightening elements there, but also uncensored truth, spirit, and originality. Gerhard Adler writes:

> For the unconscious is, as Jung has so often pointed out . . . the really potent and creative layer of our psyche [and] contains all the factors which are necessary for the integration of the personality. It possesses a superior knowledge of our real needs in regard to their integration and the ways to achieve them. Only when the unconscious is understood . . . as the "objective psyche," containing all the regulating and compensating factors which work for the wholeness of the personality, does it make sense to advise a patient to face his unconscious in . . . a direct and forceful manner.[6]

The unconscious has proven to be an invaluable source for many. My mother, for one, would often go to sleep with that day's problem on her mind and wake up in the morning with the solution. Similarly, Steve Mardeusz trusted the introverted process, though he didn't have a term for it. He could put a math problem aside and the solution would be much closer at hand when he took it up again a few hours later. I've noticed that when I'm away from the piano a few days, the next time I practice, the piece I was working on has magically improved. My unconscious has been teaching my fingers behind my back.

> When I decide arbitrarily that this chapter should not be too unwieldy, must not get out of hand, that it should be 67 typewritten pages, then to my amazement when I've finished the chapter I look at the page number, and it's page 67! It's a mystery to me how it happens. —*Selden Rodman, writer and poet*[7]

Creativity Expressed

> I don't play for the audience, I play for myself.
> —*Sviatoslav Richter, great introverted pianist*

Artists, writers, and composers give expression to inner images and symbols. In experiencing their work, we sometimes adopt these unconscious contents as our own. Author Isaac Bashevis Singer said, "The most important duty of a writer is to find what is really his story, his particular story, his unique story." This applies to all the arts. If you are convinced that only you can write your particular story or paint your particular painting, you have come upon something very important.

Pianist Alfred Brendel, probably an introvert, believes performing music is all about one's inner world and has dedicated his life to exploring the inner worlds of Mozart, Beethoven, and Schubert. His playing and his personality are discussed in these excerpts from a *New Yorker* article by A. Alvarez:

> He has a wonderful grasp of the structure of each piece, of the way it develops emotionally as well as intellectually, and this makes his playing strangely inward, as though he were following the composer's own train of thought and enabling the audience to share in the act of creation. . . . His music is like his

USING THE PSYCHOLOGICAL PREFERENCES IN MUSIC*

Performing classical music uses the functions simultaneously by calling on:

introverted feeling to respond emotionally to music and make judgments about how to perform it.

extraverted feeling to communicate feeling and style to the audience.

introverted thinking for analyzing the form and historical style.

extraverted thinking for communicating these elements to the audience.

introverted sensation to apply one's inner life to subjectively interpret the music.

extraverted sensation to communicate the sound and style clearly and objectively.

introverted intuition for insights into the structure of the music and imagining possible interpretations.

extraverted intuition to express oneself and to be creative; for spontaneity, as if the performer is making up the music as she goes along.

* See Chapter 8 for more information about the Myers-Briggs system for measuring psychological preferences.

painting and his poetry: each is a separate world with its own reasons and its own rewards, in which he can also find out about himself.[8]

Violinist and psychologist Annemarie Sudermann suggests that extraverted writers and artists like to talk, have people around them, and enjoy seeking help from friends and resources.

USING THE ENNEAGRAM IN MUSIC

Performing classical music uses all nine styles simultaneously by calling on:

The perfectionist (1) for discipline, principles of style, and expressing exactness, clarity, and drive.

The helper (2) for a harmonizing attitude when playing with other musicians, and expressing tender feelings, love, and relatedness.

The achiever (3) for working hard and expressing high energy, quickness, and perpetual motion.

The romantic (4) for heartfelt communication with the audience; for expressing a wide range of emotions, including beauty, tragedy, and longing.

The observer (5) for music analysis and applying sensitivity, subtlety, and nuance.

The questioner (6) for keen listening or alertness, musical intelligence, loyalty to the musical group, and expressing nervousness, anxiety, and conflict when they are expressed in the music.

The adventurer (7) for expressing quickness, humor, joy, lightness, enthusiasm, and playfulness.

The asserter (8) for a no-nonsense attitude and decisiveness concerning repertoire, style, and expression; for expressing anger and power in the music.

The peacemaker (9) for perceiving the whole orchestra, all the registers of a piano, or all the voices of a fugue; for mellow, sweet, or pastoral feelings.

"They find their deepest self when they're *doing*. And the part they have to do alone helps introduce them to solitude."

Michael Frayns and other authors have said that novelists feel comfortable being inside their characters, but dramatists see the characters from the outside. There may be more introverted novelists than dramatists.

As for actors:

A well-known actor was being interviewed recently on the subject of actors in politics. The interview made reference to several actors or former actors who had gained important elective offices.

And then the interviewer asked, "Do you think actors should enter politics?" The actor thought about this for a moment, and then replied, "I think that an actor, like any other . . . should take an interest in government. But as far as running for office, I don't think that is a good idea, because actors are essentially introverts, while politicians are essentially extraverts." He was then asked how he could consider a [person] who continually faces an audience to be an introvert. To this he answered, "In acting, one's greatest concern is placing oneself into the role of the character; that means one has to let the feeling of that character affect you, you have to live it in a very personal way from your own insides. This requires knowing yourself, for unless you know yourself you cannot really know another person. Actually the audience is a relatively unimportant consideration to actors as they master their role. But with politicians it is all different. There the game is to conquer the crowd. Playing the part is incidental." —*June Singer*[9]

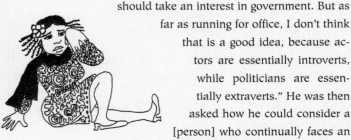

How Introverts and Extraverts Differ Concerning Creativity

It is essential for extraverts to bring their feelings out
and express them; otherwise they don't know they
have the feelings. Introverts don't have this need
and often seem to be hiding things.
—*Liz Ratcliffe, therapist*

The path of creativity moves from passive to active, and introverts tend to express themselves in more passive ways (but not always!); they generally process information slowly, deliberately, and narrowly, which carries over into the way they express their creativity. For example, Princeton professor (and introvert) Andrew Wiles spent seven years working alone and in secret solving the proof of Fermat's Last Theorem, considered the world's most difficult mathematical problem. Only an introvert could endure this much seclusion.

With Savannah, she associates her ability to feel deeply with being uncomfortable socially. So she expresses the way social interactions affect her by writing poetry.

Sally's extraverted friend Milé just can't understand this desire for inward creative release. Since extraverted Milé never hesitates to share his thoughts, feelings, and latest creative work with his friends, he can't understand why Sally rarely invites him into her rich inner world. This isn't intentional on Sally's part. She and other introverts just tend to share their worlds less frequently than most extraverts.

One of the lessons we can learn from introverts is the value many of them place on truth:

> At the age of 14 I fell into one of those fits of bottomless despair which come with adolescence because of the mediocrity of my natural faculties . . . . What I minded was not the lack of external successes but having no hope of access to that transcendent realm where only the truly great can enter and where truth dwells. I felt it better to die than to live without truth. — *Simone Weil*[10]

While most introverts choose passive expressions of their creativity, extraverts prefer the active mode.

> Music is such a vehicle to the inner part of me. —*Harriet Glaser*

> I'm a very gregarious kind of guy, and I do my science in a gregarious fashion . . . I don't work alone so well [and] I really need someone else working with me who presents new ideas . . . . —*Paul Saltman, molecular chemist*[11]

Biologist Knute Fisher hates to waste time being unproductive. "Pondering is good," he says, "but only for as long as it takes to come up with a 'doing' solution. It is useful as an energy 'push' to get something done." After Dr. Fisher does creative research, he prepares to show the results to his colleagues by asking himself, "Will it be accepted? Is it really good?"

Sam Glaser, a composer and entertainer in his early forties, can't stand wasting time. He's "on" or "holding court" almost constantly, including concerts every weekend. Being forced to wait without a book to read or his CD player to listen to is an "unmitigated torture; like a quickening death," he says. Every moment of his life has to count. He's got to get it all done and make a mark.

> I almost never take [a vacation] because the work itself has tremendous relaxation for me even when I'm under pressure . . . I love being in it. I love to talk about it when I'm not doing it in the evening . . . I don't feel I want to get away from it. [Directing] can be done as a totally autocratic method and work brilliantly . . . I'm not constituted that way. I do it on the other level of getting everyone's motor going on my tempo, on my enthusiasm, on my energy; people often say that they're more exhausted after working with me than ever before, because they were working at a higher tempo and a higher emotional pitch.
> —*Sidney Lumet, movie director*[12]

Mihaly Csikszentmihaly explains why some extraverts have trouble experiencing flow:

> Keeping order in the mind from within is very difficult. We need external goals, external stimulation, external feedback to keep attention directed. And when external input is lacking, attention begins to wander, and thoughts become chaotic . . . With nothing to do, the mind is unable to prevent negative thoughts from elbowing their way to center stage . . . Worries about one's love life, health, investments, family, and job are always hovering at the periphery of attention, waiting until there is nothing pressing that demands concentration. As soon as the mind is ready to relax, zap! The potential problems that were waiting in the wings take over.[13]

How to Coax the Creative Process

Opportunity favors the prepared mind.
—Knute Fisher

You cannot turn on inspiration and the introverted process at will, but you can prepare to be creative by learning skills, studying up, and getting enough rest. Notice when you feel most inspired: first thing in the morning, on vacations, or in the shower, for example.

Remember, your enthusiasm for a project shows that you are already unconsciously invested in it! Flexibility is important, too; for some people, listening to music frees the mind for being receptive to new ideas. Also, creating is more fulfilling when you can tolerate ambiguity and failure. Here are a few other suggestions:

STUDY THE LIVES OF CREATIVE PEOPLE.   Many of the creative geniuses we have heard about have made creativity their life's work, often putting it above relationships, family, and money. They follow hunches, give their fantasies free reign, try new things without knowing whether they'll pay off or not, and are willing to examine almost anything for its potential. Rules can be broken. Other duties can be ignored. According to Albert Einstein, "The most beautiful thing we can experience is the mysterious. It is the source of all true art and science."[14]

Robert Engman works at his craft every day, if at all possible: "Whenever I don't work with consistency I'm impossible to live with. I'm not kind to my family. I get wrapped up in all sorts of complications. As long as I work as a sculptor I'm straight and honest and unafraid . . . It has to be peculiarly related to a measurement of myself to myself."[15]

Movie director Mike Nichols understands that the most unacknowledged part of creativity is the unconscious down time. "A lousy day is as important as a good day because the subconscious is still at work."

Arthur Koestler, social scientist and writer, talks about the importance of not getting side-tracked: "Depression might be creative. Elation might be creative. What's important in mood is not to be deflected, obsessed with anything outside the work. So, it's an eliminatory process of your defenses against extraneous matter."[16]

LISTEN TO YOUR HEART. Sometimes we approach a new project feeling lukewarm about it. We do our best, however, when we can hear our heart beating with passion for our work and should learn to take full advantage of these inspired moments.

Introverted Stephen Kresge was writing a book on economics and not enjoying it. It would annoy him that the idea he was concentrating on would be replaced by a new idea—then he would forget one or both of them. So he put the project aside out of frustration. After some years, he found himself writing a lighter kind of work based on his fantasies. There was no forgetting—only a sense of flow, freedom, and delight in what he was doing.

I am in my work like a pit in its fruit.

—Rilke

As Kresge himself put it, "The hard shell of reality dissolved and all these possibilities streamed in." After this, he vowed that he would only do projects in which his heart and soul were fully engaged. (This is not meant to imply that the flow experience cannot be attached to writing about facts.)

Some people create according to a rigid schedule. Others wait for the spirit to move them. Composer Aaron Copland said, "If I feel in the mood to write, something starts me off. I might feel sad. I might feel lonely. I might feel elated. I might have gotten a good letter from somebody."[17]

Life events can motivate creativity, as they did fashion designer Bonnie Cashin:

> Sometimes intense emotional happenings have had the effect of intensifying creative action . . . When my mother died, which was a terrible shock to me, I applied myself with great intensity to working, and also turned to studies of a spiritual nature. The period was, in retrospect, one of strong creativity, accomplishment, and growth. Perhaps the creative person uses problems in a constructive way. Maybe this is what life is all about.[18]

SCHEDULE IN QUIET TIME.   This can take place in a special part of your home or in a natural setting.

> I know that it is extremely important to be alone for a time, to have a time and place apart; to be . . . away from the mainland, away from the scheduled interactive life, away from other people's energies, needs, and projections. I found that solitude gives me myself for company, and that when I am alone, especially in the early morning, it is as if I am a deep quiet pool that allows whatever needs to come into my awareness to surface.
> —*Writer Jean Shinoda Bolen, probably an introvert*[19]

WORK WITH YOUR DREAMS.   Communicate with your unconscious by writing your dreams down and drawing them—your drawing skill is unimportant. Imagine the dream continuing; if you dream about a hall with closed doors, for example, open them and see where they take you. Also, think about each character and item as representing a part of yourself.

BE OPEN TO ACCIDENTS.   We've all heard of great scientific discoveries, such as penicillin, that were the result of an accident. When something doesn't go as planned, fascinating new possibil-

ities often come into view. Here's a glimpse into how fashion designer Bonnie Cashin operates:

> Sometimes I'll take everything out of the closets, throw
> them on the floor, try on certain things, maybe upside down or
> wrong things together, and all of a sudden a certain juxtaposi-
> tion looks absolutely marvelous. And thus may start a whole
> trend of new designs. It's an accident; yet I wonder if the acci-
> dent was meant to be. Free association, free experiment, it's all
> part of the play thing. That's why I love to spatter paint around,
> cut rashly into fabric, pile up shapes in clay, throw the body
> about to some loud music. It's part of creative play.[20]

SOMETIMES IT TAKES A TEAM.   Your team can be made up
of parts of yourself at different ages: remember what in your childhood gave you a sense of wonder and magic. Take special note if
a child appears in your dreams to guide you.

Introverted Chase had talent and perseverance and loved
writing songs, but he wasn't attracted to the business end of being
an entertainer. His extraverted friend, Robin, however, was a
good entrepreneur and determined to become famous. When the
two of them started a band, Robin got them gigs. By helping

Chase make use of his talent, Robin achieved her dream of fame and Chase got to do what he liked best.

Extraverts, especially, may prefer group efforts. Movie director Sidney Lumet, for one, states,

> I find that when we're working I want us to get away, live together, be together. I just finished a picture this fall, *The Sea Gull*, which from a working point of view is the most exciting experience I ever had and probably one of the things that made it so exciting was that we were isolated in Sweden. . . . It was a genuine communal family life, living together, eating together, and working together. It turned out for me the most rewarding work experience I've ever had.[21]

Paul Saltman, a molecular chemist, claims, "I don't like to sit alone. I don't like to see very quiet places. I like to see them in a state of creative dynamism."[22]

Many introverts prefer to work behind the scenes. According to W. Novak and Moshe Waloks, "Lenny Bruce . . . grew up in an entirely assimilated household on Long Island; his Jewish education, such as it was, and his knowledge of Yiddish words were both acquired in his mid-twenties from fellow comic Joe Ancis, a legendary New Yorker who is said to be too shy to perform publicly, but who has influenced many successful comedians."[23]

Some of us tap into both the introverted and extraverted sides of ourselves. Here is Carl Jung's description of his own amazingly creative personality:

> Somewhere deep in the background I always knew that I was two persons. One [the extravert] was the son of my parents, who went to school and was less intelligent, attentive, hard working, decent, and clean than many other boys.
>
> The other [the introvert] was grown up—old, in fact, skeptical, mistrustful, remote from the world of men, but close to nature, the earth, the sun, the moon, the weather, all living creatures, and above all close to the night, to dreams, and to

CREATIVITY QUIZ

(Answer T for "true" and F for "false")

1. We cannot know another's internal experience, but we can sometimes get close to it through poetry and novels.
2. Introverts tend to prefer listening to CDs that consist of music by one composer, one musician, or one piece of music. Extraverts often prefer a variety of composers, artists, and compositions.
3. Taking in a museum exhibit alone is an extraverted experience.
4. Though you might not feel creatively inspired, after you start in you might become energized about your project.
5. Flow experiences are never accompanied by feelings of well-being or feeling at one with the cosmos.
6. Only those with immense talent or gigantic brains can be creative.
7. While most monuments are tall and showy, the "wall" at the Vietnam Veterans Memorial in Washington, DC, is designed in a more subtle and introverted style.
8. People might have trouble being creative if they're too obsessed with themselves.
9. It's good to paint, draw, or make up cartoons—even if the result is kind of silly.

ANSWERS:

1. true; 2. true; 3. false; 4. true; 5. false; 6. false; 7. true; 8. true; 9. true

Fleaquined Fryer

whatever "god" worked directly in him. . . . Besides in his world there existed another realm, like a temple in which anyone who entered was transformed and suddenly overpowered by a vision of the whole cosmos, so that he could only marvel and admire, forgetful of himself. Here lived the "Other," who knew God as a hidden, personal, and at the same time suprapersonal secret. Here nothing separated man from God; indeed, it was as though the human mind looked down upon Creation simultaneously with God.

I was not conscious of this in any articulate way, though I sensed it with an overpowering premonition and intensity of feeling. At such times I knew I was worthy of myself, that I was my true self. As soon as I was alone, I could pass over into this state. I therefore sought the peace and solitude of the "Other," personality Number Two.[24]

6

Dr. Carl Gustav Jung and Introversion/ Extraversion

My life is the self-realization of the unconscious.
—C. G. Jung

Carl Gustav Jung (1875–1961), who was born in Switzerland and eventually died there, spent much of his life in Vienna. He was not the first person to talk about introversion and extraversion— these terms were used as far back as the 1600s—but he was the first to see them as basic psychological dimensions. An introvert as well as a brilliant psychiatrist and scholar, Jung devoted his life to understanding the psyche. His astute observation and his study of anthropology, comparative religion, philosophy, and archaeology led him to the discovery of universals in human nature. As a psychiatrist, he found ways the resources of the unconscious could be used—not only to heal those with troubled lives, but also to help healthy or "normal" people live more spiritually and creatively.

Jung noticed the introverted and extraverted sides of his own personality when he was a boy, naming them "number one" and "number two." As an old man, his recollection of inner experiences grew more and more vivid, while his memories of outer experiences faded. "Only what is interior has proved to have substance," he said.

As a result of powerful religious childhood visions and dreams, Jung came to fervently believe that one's relationship with God should be personal and experiential. This separated him from his church and his clergyman father, who insisted that believing in God be a matter of blind faith.

Jung was on his way to becoming a medical doctor when suddenly, in a burst of intuition, he decided to go into psychiatry:

> Here alone the two currents of my interest could flow together and in a united stream dig their own bed. Here was the empirical field common to biological and spiritual facts, which I had everywhere sought and nowhere found. Here at last was the place where the collision of nature and spirit became a reality.[1]

Jung and Freud

Freud had taught me that everybody is somewhat neurotic, and that we must practice tolerance. But I was not at all inclined to content myself with that; rather, I wanted to know how one could escape having a neurosis.
—C. G. Jung[2]

Sigmund Freud (1856–1939), along with Jung, believed that scientists would one day integrate the psychological and physiological aspects of the psyche. This is confirmed by current neurological and biochemical research. Freud, a strong-willed and authoritarian neurologist and physician, was the founder of psychoanalysis and one of the first to try to understand mental illness instead of dismissing it. Unlike Jung, however, he promoted the theory that symptoms are wishes relating to infantile sexuality.

Freud was writing his famous *Interpretation of Dreams* at the same time Jung was finishing medical school. Several years after their first meeting (which lasted 13 hours), Jung reported, "I found him extremely intelligent and shrewd, yet my first impressions of him remained somewhat tangled; I could not make him out." Jung valued dreams as the most direct link to the unconscious and living realities that can teach and heal. He did not buy Freud's dream theory: "I was never able to agree with Freud that the dream is a "facade" behind which its meaning lies hidden—a meaning already known but maliciously, so to speak, withheld from consciousness."[3]

Jung felt that Freud had substituted sexuality for God. Therefore, Freud's attempts to force the younger man to accept his ideas, and even to promote them as dogma, were unsuccessful. This important relationship, and their subsequent split, motivated Jung to become interested in personality types.

> . . . Freud's view of the unconscious as a murky pond that
> could be drained by analysis and redeveloped by the ego in the

Unconscious

service of a purely rational consciousness was bitterly uncongenial to Jung: [Jung] regarded an exclusively rational view of human nature as hopelessly inadequate. The profound experiences of psychological transformation involved in the development of personality depended more on irrational than rational processes, and any psychology which failed to grant due honor to these processes would be a betrayal of mankind . . . In the unconscious, Jung believed, there resided the collective wisdom of our species. . . . —*Dr. Anthony Stevens*[4]

Archetypes

One of Jung's major contributions to depth psychology was his research on universal or primordial images called *archetypes*, inborn patterns in the structure of the psyche that represent form without content. Archetypes lay dormant in the *collective unconscious*, a part of the unconscious that people spanning all times and cultures share, and become filled in as we live our lives. Though they exert a powerful influence on us, we do not have conscious, direct contact with them.

Anima

The *personal unconscious* refers to those aspects of our individual lives that are hidden from the *ego*, the ego being

Trickster

Villain

Mystic

Martyr

Spiritual leader

Mother

Wise man

Warrior

Solitary

Lover

Hero

Magician

Shadow

King

examples of archetypes

that which we know as "I." There is no clear dividing line between the personal and collective unconscious:

> . . . In the psychological material brought up by individu-
> als, the personal material shows the effects of its collective
> background. Each succeeding level of the unconscious may be
> thought of as going deeper and becoming more collective in its
> nature. The wonder of the collective unconscious is that it is all
> there, all the legend and history of the human race, with its un-
> exorcised demons and its gentle saints, its mysteries and its
> wisdom, all within each one of us . . . The exploration of this
> world is more challenging than the exploration of the solar sys-
> tem. —*June Singer*[5]

The Shadow

Jung's innovations, including
his insights into psychological type, were products of
his quest for balance and
wholeness. Integrating the
shadow, which includes archetypes and other elements, is
an essential part of this quest.

According to Jung: "The shadow represents first and foremost the
personal unconscious, [whose] contents can be made conscious.
In this it differs from the contents of the collective unconscious,
which are much further from consciousness and in normal circumstances are seldom if ever realized."[6]

Jung defined the shadow as all of the unconscious.
Sometimes we have a vague sense of the shadow when we make
slips of the tongue or get uncomfortable feelings we don't understand. The shadow is also represented by dark figures in dreams.
It isn't only a place where negative things are stored. Anything we
repress goes there, such as talents, gifts, and abilities we're not

able to own, and negative characteristics we don't accept about ourselves.

> What we cannot admit in ourselves we often find in others. If a person—who speaks of another person whom he hates with a vengeance that seems nearly irrational—can be brought to describe the characteristics which he most dislikes, you will frequently have a picture of his own repressed aspects which are unrecognized by him though obvious to others. —*June Singer*[7]

Jung believed that "no one can become conscious of the shadow without considerable moral effort. This act is the essential condition for self-knowledge, and it therefore, as a rule, meets with considerable resistance."

If one attitude is conscious, the opposite recedes to a less conscious, shadowy place. If introverts think of themselves as nothing but reliable, peaceful, and calm, for example, they will struggle with shadow elements that are unreliable, warlike, and agitated. If extraverts think of themselves as highly adventurous,

A man and his shadow.

carefree, and daring, they may come up against shadow forces that are overly cautious, moody, and timid.

PROJECTING THE SHADOW

Attributing our own unacknowledged wishes, feelings, or characteristics to others is called *projection*.

> Overreaction, overkill, and excessive emotion are sure signs that something unconscious has been touched and is finding expression. When people overreact to something in another person they are casting their own Shadow on that person. That which people most vociferously and emotionally despise in others is most surely that which is there in themselves of which they are completely unconscious. The offense one most rages against out there in another may look very different in oneself because each of us has our own style. Yet, at root something will be the same. One projects on others that which one most dislikes in oneself. —*Anne Brennan*[8]

An alcoholic I know has an unrealistic view of herself as nothing but "good." When she rants about how horrible "those" alcoholics are, she is disavowing her own flaw and attributing it

to others. She projects her shame away from herself, for it is too painful to own. In the process of becoming whole, we recognize and take responsibility for our shadow. Each shadow issue we reclaim is one less to project out onto another person, nationality, or race.

EXAMPLES OF INTROVERTS AND EXTRAVERTS AS EACH OTHER'S SHADOW

> . . . Extraverts project their weaknesses on introverts and introverts project their inferior side on extraverts. The one who moves easily and without hesitation into and through the world of objects is called "shallow" and "pushy." The one who is in contact with the inner psychic realm is called "inscrutable" and "slow."
> —*Anne Brennan*[9]

• Jason, a high school student, has repressed his introverted side due to strong family pressure. He distances himself from the quiet and thoughtful aspects of his personality and projects them onto those "lame" schoolmates who are studious.

• Twelve-year-old Elsa denies being attracted to high-profile social activities out of fear that her introverted and withdrawn parents might reject her for being different from them. She projects this unlived potential onto outgoing classmates and criticizes them as "social butterflies."

• Delia held securely onto her introverted nature even though her extraverted parents "treated her like a green and yellow parrot" and kept prodding her to show off. Outside of home, she was able to develop serious and thoughtful relationships that suited her personality.

• The media likes to feature titillating shadow stories about the lives of "weird" introverts, like movie star James Dean. While this brooding loner is a shadow figure to most extraverts, he is a known entity to introverts who recognize his characteristics in themselves.

• Another representative of mainstream America's shadow is soft-spoken and shy George Lucas, the *Star Wars* mogul.

> "I'm not the kind of person who'd jump into a crowd of people I don't know and say, 'Hi, I'm George, glad to meet you. I'm from Modesto, where are you from?'" he said. Lucas accuses the media of overplaying his introversion and turning him into 'a pathologically shy, reclusive, Howard Hughes–like freak that can't be touched by people.'"— *Edward Guthmann*[10]

• Jung tried to dispel his culture's belief that introverts are self-centered and strange. As an old man looking back upon his life, he talked about a part of himself he had kept in the shadow so others wouldn't think he was eccentric:

> . . . I was held back by a secret fear that I might perhaps be like him [Nietzsche], at least in regard to the "secret" which had isolated him from his environment. Perhaps—who knows?—he had had inner experiences, insights which he had unfortunately talked about, and had found out that no one understood him.
>
> Obviously he was, or at least was considered to be, an eccentric, a sport of nature, which I did not want to be under any circumstances. I feared that I might be forced to recognize that I too was such a strange bird.[11]

Jung was curious, open-minded, and eager to look at anything that might help explain the mysteries of the human psyche and spirit.

He also had the precious and uncanny ability to hold that two opposites can both be true.

Many psychotherapists practicing today have been trained in the Jungian tradition. Let me encourage you to read books by Jung and those who have been trained or otherwise influenced by him: James Hillman, Marian Woodmont, Robert Johnson, Alice Miller, Paul Tillich, Alan Watts, Aldous Huxley, Marie-Louise von Franz, Erik Fromm, June Singer, and Rollo May, among others.

Another example of Jung's legacy is the 12-step movement adopted by such programs as Alcoholics Anonymous and AlAnon. The founders of these programs learned from Jung

119

INTROVERSION/EXTRAVERSION QUIZ

(Answer T for "true" and F for "false")

1. Individuation or self-realization is essentially an extraverted process.
2. Archetypes are psychic patterns that recur in different cultures and times. Instincts are built-in behaviors.
3. The collective unconscious houses archetypes. The personal unconscious houses the shadow and individual experiences. There is no clear-cut dividing line between them.
4. To Jung, awareness of the shadow provides insight into the many-sidedness of our own nature. Without the shadow reminding us, we might see ourselves as only black or white, good or bad.
5. In dreams, the shadow figure is usually the same sex as the dreamer.
6. All shadow elements are the same distance from consciousness.
7. Jung believed that neuroses and psychoses arise from the conflict between our instinctive natures and the pressures of society for us to not be ourselves.
8. Jung had nothing to do with introducing Eastern religion to the West.
9. Introverts never implode or freeze when stressed. Extraverts never explode or become hysterical when stressed.
10. Introverts often like to read books where they can experience others' inner worlds.
11. Jung and Freud were good buddies all of their lives.

ANSWERS:
1. false; 2. true; 3. true; 4. true; 5. true; 6. false; 7. true; 8. false; 9. false; 10. true; 11. false

that we cannot change unwanted habits purely by means of our ego or will.

7

Neurology and Personality

Introversion and extraversion describe behaviors that begin early—often in infancy—and in most cases do not change significantly. Of all our personality traits, these seem the most closely related to genetics. Parents who pressure their children to behave against their in-born temperaments put their children at risk for growing up disturbed.

In Jung's day, most scientists believed babies were blank slates waiting to be filled in by their environment. More and more evidence supports Dr. Jung's belief, however, that the psyche is as biologically based as our physical properties. Some of the characteristics and attitudes we keep through life are connected to the way our brains were wired before we came into the world. These include how receptive and intelligent we are, our facility with language, and whether we are inclined to be neurotic or stable, agreeable or grouchy, introverted or extraverted. The way we are made up genetically interacts with environmental factors, causing continual changes within our brains.

If we don't like something about our lives, we can try to do something about it. We may not be able to simply *will* ourselves to be different, but since our brains are plastic and able to create new cells that wire themselves into functional circuits, it's worthwhile for us to present ourselves with long-range challenges. For example, I am an INFP (introverted, intuitive, feeling, perceiving type) in the Myers-Briggs system of personality identification. I have never tried to change from this usually quiet type to its opposite—I don't think I could, nor would I want to. But many years ago I decided to try to become more comfortable around people. So I persisted in making more friends and got used to being with them regularly. After a few years, I noticed my experiment was working because I felt less nervous socially.

When Did Introversion and Extraversion Begin?

Could introverts and extraverts have been differentiated this far back?

Around two million years ago, our brains increased in size as we became more flexible and adaptive to handle severe climate changes. Roughly 50,000 to 120,000 years ago, distinctions be-

tween introverts and extraverts evolved as we spread out of Africa into other parts of the world.

Although only humans have a highly developed preference for introversion and extraversion, other animals, including dogs and cats, show some signs of them as well. As with many introverted humans, Penny's dog Lizzie, a serious gopher hunter, is single-minded and territorial.

Don's shepherd Digger's behavior resembles that of many extraverts. He's responsive to his companions, energetic, and optimistic, and can quickly shift his attention over a broad area.

As with many introverted humans, most cats seem aloof and indifferent to majority opinion, though examples of the opposite can be found.

Many of us introverts are especially sensitive to loud noises, bright lights, and crowded rooms. If our sense of smell were as sensitive as Lizzie's, the odors of a whole room full of people would probably overwhelm us. The Diggers among us, however, might find the variety exciting and fascinating.

As we humans look for balance, we can learn some things from the worlds of dogs and cats. First, we all have both doglike and catlike tendencies to draw upon. Second, it would do each of us good to have a dog that worships us and a cat that ignores us.

Measurable Differences in Humans

> The extravert does not dwell in images connected to emotions and previous experiences, but flits in and out, from matching associations (with little or no mulling or ruminating time) to reaction. This would hold with the evolutionary view of needing a small number of ponderers and a large number of fast reactors.
> —John Weber, an extravert

When young men and women, who were shy as children, were exposed to stresses such as harsh smells and then measured in a laboratory, their heart rates stayed elevated longer than that of their outgoing peers. Dr. Jerome Kagan found that timid children's sympathetic nervous systems are more easily aroused; they exhibit higher blood pressure when at rest, greater dilation of their pupils, and higher levels of norepinephrine markers in their urine.[1]

Since introverts are on higher alert internally than extraverts, they have greater blood flow in their brains, experience lower pain thresholds, and need more sedatives to fall asleep. Introverts are sometimes referred to as "diminishers" because they are easily overwhelmed by outside stimulation. Extraverts raise their level of stimulation by seeking excitement, behaving impulsively, and taking chances.

In addition to the neurological differences noted on page 75 in Chapter 4, other research shows that:

- introverts' performances on complex cognitive tasks are more negatively affected by music and noise than extraverts', with music being as distracting as noise.[2]
- when people exchange favors, heightened neural activity is displayed in areas of the brain that process rewards and detect others' intentions. These surges of good feeling may explain why extraverts, especially, like to work with others.[3]
- a chemistry in part of the limbic area of the brain causes small babies to be sensitive to unfamiliar, discrepant, or novel events. Those with a low threshold to react (often introverts) respond to mobiles and smells by thrashing and crying. When they become toddlers, what are unfamiliar are not smells and sights, but other people.[4]
- introverts report significantly more vividness in mental imagery than extraverts after listening to stories.[5]
- there are biological reasons for some of the introverted and extraverted ways people behave when they communicate.[6]
- in Japan, children with high introversion or high intellect were found to have stronger influences from family environment than those with high extraversion or low intellect.[7] (If a similar study were made in the U.S., it is unlikely that it would yield the same results.)
- subjects whose scores were higher on the Eysenck Personality Inventory Extroversion scale tolerated pain longer.[8]
- A growing body of psychophysiological evidence points to the possibility that individual differences in early auditory

processing contributes to social withdrawal and introverted tendencies.[9]

- In a study of milk production and farmers' personality types, the cows of introverted farmers yielded more milk than the cows of farmers with a preference for extraversion.[10]

The Brain and Introversion

The *cerebrum* accounts for 85 percent of our brain's weight and is the site of memories, understanding, perceiving, planning, initiating movement, and generating and inhibiting behavior. Increasing the cerebrum's cognitive activity helps lessen social anxiety.

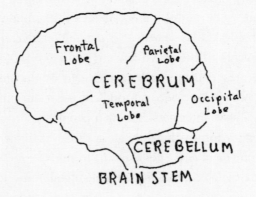

The *frontal lobe* is the center of personality and emotional traits. It enables typically introverted activities, such as keeping track of history and studying, and typically extraverted activities, such as leading and taking direct action.

The *limbic system* (also called the *midbrain*) includes the *thalamus, hypothalamus, amygdala,* and *hippocampi*. This system processes stress reactions. When shy people feel threatened in social situations, fear and reluctance to take action causes their mouths to become dry and their jaws to lock up. The amygdala is thought to be the seat of emotions, emotional memory, and the region of the fight-or-flight response. By telling the brain to make the senses more alert, it responds to anything new, emergency situations, and certain stimuli that never reach consciousness.

Introverts who have trouble thinking when put on the spot may be in the grip of their amygdala. Worrying that their shyness or slowness to respond is not acceptable to others only increases their anxiety. Extraverts' thinking, however, is often sharpened rather than impaired in social situations. Since their nervous systems tend to be less vulnerable to overstimulation, less stands in the way of their actions and speech. Whether introverts freeze or run from uncomfortable social situations depends on which part of the brain the amygdala has projected messages onto.

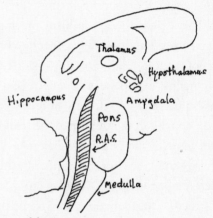

BRAIN STEM

According to Daniel Goleman:

> Those prone to fearfulness are born with a neurochemistry that makes the neural circuit centered on the amygdala easily aroused, so they avoid the unfamiliar, shy away from uncertainty, and suffer anxiety. Most extraverts have a higher thresh-

old for amygdala arousal and are less easily frightened, more naturally outgoing, and therefore eager to explore new places and meet new people.[11]

The *brain stem* is in charge of the functions and basic instincts that keep us alive. Information from sight, hearing, taste, and touch moves through the brain stem, passes through the limbic system (where smell is added), and then into the cortex (where we think about it).

The *reticular activating system* (RAS) is a complex of neural pathways that alerts the cortex to arriving information by way of the thalamus, which can inhibit or amplify messages. This regulates levels of arousal and activity. The more active the RAS, the more able we are to focus attention on outside events. According to Dr. James Newman, the upper segment of the RAS is related to introversion. This "closed-loop" arousal mechanism connects neurons in the cortex with internally generated brain states. The lower segment of the RAS relates to extraversion through connecting the sense organs' experiences of outer events to the brain's rapid responses. The fact that activity in one section of the RAS tends to cut off activity in the other may be related to individual preferences for introversion and extraversion.[12]

Whenever we think, feel, or move, neural pathways throughout our whole brain are involved. We owe our individuality to the microscopic structure and functioning of approximately 100 billion brain cells, called neurons, that connect with each other by means of billions of links, called *synapses*. Electricity enables chemical messages (neurotransmitters) to jump across the liquid-filled synapses between them. According to brain expert Joseph LeDoux, "It's practically a truism to say the synapses underlie personality since synapses underlie everything the brain does."[13] Both nature and nurture contribute to the wiring of synapses in the brain.

It can be soothing to know that introverts and extraverts have different interests because of their different genes and brain structures. Our most basic personality traits are unlikely to change. In healthy people, however, neuronal wiring is plastic enough to accommodate self-improvements and growth at almost any age. Developing our creativity by involving both the intellectual and emotional parts of the brain, discussing our experiences with others, and developing a practice of meditation or talking positively to ourselves.

Genetics

Though much progress has taken place over the past 150 years, genetics is still in its youth. Gene therapy—treating, curing, or preventing defects by changing the expression of a person's

genes—is in its infancy and primarily experimental. The following projects promise major advances in physical and mental health care and may contribute useful findings related to introversion/extraversion and other aspects of personality:

• The Human Genome Project, begun formally in 1990, maps our 20,000–25,000 genes, and aims to determine the sequences of the 3 billion chemical base pairs that make up human DNA, store this information, and address ethical, legal, and social issues concerning DNA. Knowing the sequence may help establish a genetic basis for introversion/extraversion.

• The Brain Molecular Anatomy Project (BMAP) catalogs genes at different developmental stages, with special focus on the mouse's brain. Its database promises to screen for individuals who might be at risk for developing brain disorders.

• The International HapMap Project, whose name comes from genes that are passed down in large blocks (haplotypes),

Don't be so sure, Mom.

studies how people diverge from the average. This may include extreme introverts and extreme extraverts.

If children are known to have certain sets of genes, careful monitoring of their environments may be able to prevent severe personality problems such as social phobia in introverts and overaggression in extraverts. It is already known that:

• In a study by Dr. Marco Battaglia, 49 shy third- and fourth-grade children were found to have one or two shorter copies of a gene that codes for the flow of the brain chemical serotonin.[14]

• Research supports the contention that extraverts have a more positive communicator image and that communication behavior has biological aspects.[15]

• The dopamine receptor gene, DRD4, is associated with novelty seeking and related measures of extraversion.[16] Males with a reduced level of another gene, MAOA, which elevates levels of mood-regulating neurotransmitters, are sometimes unusually sensation seeking and impulsive and may emerge from an abusive childhood engaging in violent behavior. Males with a

similar background but normal levels of MAOA are less affected.[17]

8

Introverts, the Workplace, and Myers-Briggs

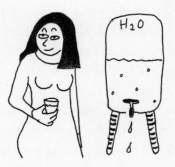

Introverts can't just walk into any job and be happy. However, by putting our knowledge about introversion and other personality traits to use, we can generate certain guidelines regarding employment that, if followed, will pay off for both employer and employee. For example, when introverted Karen applied for a job, she told her prospective employers that maybe they'd do better to hire an extraverted feeling type to conduct phone interviews and give her one of the other jobs instead. Whenever she called the office of the interview subject, she would often be passed on to the secretaries of the people she was looking for. Then, when she finally reached the person she wanted, some of her best questions wouldn't surface until 15 minutes after she'd hung up the phone. Eventually her employers paid attention to what she had been telling them and placed her in a more suitable position for an introvert: writing the in-house newsletter.

Hector, another introvert, also faced some challenges at work as a teacher. Standing in front of large history classes teaching junior high school students was stressful. The extraverted teachers, Hector noticed, were better at holding the students' attention. After three years, Hector, an introverted feeling type, transferred to another school to work with students one on one in small special-education classes. Now he felt his life had more meaning.

Personality tests such as the Myers-Briggs Type Indicator (MBTI) are useful for determining personality types. The MBTI is a thorough personality test that consists of selecting pairs of statements that best fit us. In this section, introverts especially will find tools to help them choose the appropriate occupation and work setting, as well as tips to help them get along better with employers, employees, and coworkers. In addition, some extraverts may learn that it's wise to slow down and reflect before speaking.

Sometimes Dr. Foot-in-the-Mouth wished he were more introverted, at least if that meant he'd be less likely to embarrass himself.

The Myers-Briggs (MBTI) Typology System

Katherine Cook Briggs began developing a personality typology based on the study of biographies during World War I and realized Carl Jung had a similar system to hers. Her daughter, Isabell Briggs Myers, was inspired by World War II to see what she could do to help people understand each other and thus avoid such a war from occurring again. She and her mother joined forces to produce the Myers-Briggs Type Indicator.

The MBTI measures eight psychological functions or ways of processing reality: **introversion** (I), **extraversion** (E), **sensation** (S), **intuition** (N, to distinguish it from the "I" for introversion), **feeling** (F), **thinking** (T), **perceiving** (P), and **judging** (J). It then divides people into 16 four-letter types, for example, ISFJ (introverted sensate with feeling). What happens to the other four letters? We need to remember that we couldn't get through a single day without using all eight of these functions! But the theory is complicated enough when dealing with only four at a time! The letter at the end, either J or P, points to the function that is extraverted or that we see most readily. In the type ISFJ, the J points to a judging function (feeling and thinking are judging functions), in this case feeling. P (perceiving) points to either S or N (sensing or iNtuition) for how we perceive or take in our information; J (judging) points to either F or T (feeling or thinking) for how we make judgments about that information.

ISFP INFP ESFP ENFP/ISTP INTP ESTP ENTP

The P above indicates that the most visible (extraverted) function is either sensing or intuition.

ISFJ INFJ ESFJ ENFJ/ISTJ INTJ ESTJ ENTJ

The J above indicates that the most visible (extraverted) function is either thinking or feeling.

Here the theory gets a little complicated. J or P *always* refer to the EXTRAVERTED function. It's easy when we're talking about an extravert because extraverts prefer the preference that others see most easily. For example, ESFPs favor sensing *and* show it to the world. But introverts' most extraverted preference (the one the J or P points to) is *not* their favorite. Their favorite is so precious and private it needs to be protected, so we have to search for it in the middle of the four-letter group! The middle letter that is *not* pointed to by P or J, then, is introverts' favorite or dominant.

These are the steps to use when thinking about introverts: First look for the preference they show to the world, or "extravert," by looking at the P or J (for example, for the ISFJ, the extraverted preference is F). The other preference, *introverted sensing*, will be their favorite or dominant—the one they are most comfortable using.

In self-reporting, we sometimes answer questions according to how we want to be instead of how we are, so personality tests are not 100 percent accurate. Still, the MBTI has been improved several times and the results are accurate enough to be very useful to individuals and professionals around the world who use it for business and psychological purposes.

A boss who understands introversion.

In Chapter 1, you learned which attitude you prefer in general: *introversion* or *extraversion*. In this section you'll learn about *sensation, intuition, feeling,* and *thinking,* plus *perceiving* and *judging.* Sensation and intuition are dichotomies, as are thinking and feeling. More room is given to the introverted types, since introversion is the main focus of the book.

For a catalogue or other information about the Center for Applications of Psychological Type and the Myers-Briggs Type Indicator, call 800-777-2278 or visit www.capt.org.

Sensation/Intuition

Sensation and intuition are linked together, similar to the way introversion and extraversion are paired. Sensates rely on physical, tangible information while intuitives trust their inner wisdom for processing reality.

SENSATION

Sensates trust the information, awareness, and aliveness their five senses bring. They prefer things to be literal and concrete, arrive at their conclusions by way of known facts, and are grounded in the here and now.

> The sensor looks at building materials and easily sees the city that lays immanent in them. —*Nigel Thompson*

When I was 16, my practical introverted sensate mother thought ahead a few years and looked for a new interest that could occupy her time after I left home. She developed skill in making pottery, which consumed her for most of the rest of her life.

When extraverts think ahead about transitions such as this, they often choose activities that involve being with other people.

INTROVERTED SENSATES AT WORK Introverted sensates learn useful and practical skills, attend to details, and like to see

ARE YOU A SENSATE?

Note how many statements you agree with:

1. You like working with details and facts as opposed to theories.
2. You are more realistic than imaginative.
3. You like having specific directions to follow.
4. You are practical and sensible.
5. You prefer direct contact and being grounded.
6. You like doing things with your hands (cooking, gardening, sewing, repairing, painting) or working with data.
7. You are relatively traditional minded.
8. You notice and remember your surroundings.

Sensate Augie performed a valuable service to others at his office by remembering where he had seen equipment, reports, and others' misplaced objects, even when the objects were of no particular importance to him.

9. It annoys you when others do things out of sequence.
10. When confronted with a problem, you try to solve it in a routine or proven way.
11. You want to know how much time activities will take before you undertake them.
12. You often feel suspicious of people who don't seem "down to earth."
13. You often don't trust hunches.
14. When friends dwell in the past or jump to the future, you will often bring the discussion back, or want to bring it back, to the present.

If most of the above statements apply to you, you are probably a sensate type. If few of these statements apply to you, you can try to become more versatile by consciously developing your sensate side.

tangible results. Introverted sensates' least developed and most unconscious function is *extraverted intuition*, which can unexpectedly erupt in primitive and powerful ways. When triggered by an injury that keeps them from doing the sensate activities they're used to doing, for example, their intuition may malfunction and come up with irrational paranoid fantasies instead of encouraging possibilities for the future. The inferior function can be disruptive, but adds awareness and plays an important part in the process of individuation.

Introverted sensates with _thinking_ (ISTJs) often have careers as engineers, securities analysts, statisticians, accountants, dentists, electricians, executives, lawyers, police officers, technicians, mechanics, farmers, and carpenters. While ISTJs are primarily introverted, the J at the end points to the extraverted preference, thinking. It's important to realize that we each have both introversion and extraversion in our personalities.

If you are an introverted sensate with thinking, your coworkers appreciate you for being practical, concrete, reliable, efficient, and conscientious. Your responsibility, common sense, and ability to stay in the present contribute to the workplace. You thrive when you have specific goals to work for. Plan times to relax so you don't become overwhelmed from too much work. Being aware that frivolity or highly emotional situations bother you (if they do) can help you be less reactive. You want to be able to count on others and may tend to expect too much from yourself. Appreciate yourself for following rules, adhering to schedules, and being neat. The way you express things to coworkers is important—be careful to be complimentary and encouraging.

Introverted sensates with _feeling_ (ISFJs) often have jobs as librarians, health care workers, food service workers, teachers, artists, photographers, bookkeepers, medical caregivers, dental hygienists, store employees, and secretaries. While ISFJs are primarily introverted, their feeling is extraverted. The J at the end shows us that feeling, which the ISFJ uses to judge things by, is what they show to the outside world, while their sensation is more private and personal—therefore introverted.

If you are an introverted sensate with feeling, you are valuable for being loyal, responsible, calm, and bringing harmony to the workplace. Your coworkers appreciate you for being dutiful, considerate of others, and more than willing to serve. Since everyone has a human need to serve, try to let others help you as you help them. Fight the tendency to find fault with yourself by asking for logical evaluations of your work from someone you trust. You tend to be emotionally sensitive. Asking your coworkers for facts and their objective viewpoints can provide you with the reassurance you need. Also, look for coworkers who are sympathetic.

EXTRAVERTED SENSATES AT WORK Extraverted sensates seek excitement and are upbeat, gregarious, resourceful, and active. The inferior function for extraverted sensates is *introverted intuition*. When triggered, the person may become paralyzed with obsessive unrealistic thoughts about the future.

Extraverted sensates with *thinking* (ESTPs) often have careers as managers, salespeople, marketers, politicians, sports figures, carpenters, promoters, news anchors, and law enforcers. They are good at taking charge in a crisis, persuading people, and having a good time. Here P for perceiving appears at the end, which refers to how this type takes in information. In this case, it's through the senses rather than through intuition. Extraverts show their favorite to the world, unlike introverts. Since the ESTP is most comfortable with sensation, which is extraverted, thinking is secondary and introverted.

Extraverted sensates with *feeling* (ESFPs) often have jobs as receptionists, salespeople, realtors, recreation directors, travel agents, and entertainers, as well as those that involve working with children. They spread good will, work well with people, and have the flexibility and enthusiasm to make things happen. The P tells us that sensing is their favorite and thus extraverted. Their feeling is more private and introverted.

INTUITION

All great achievements of science start
from intuitive knowledge, namely, in axioms,
from which deductions are then made.
—*Albert Einstein*[1]

Intuition often takes the form of hunches and theories in science, or fantasy, inspiration, and imagination in the arts. Intuitives often become experts in a specific area of knowledge. They are interested in new ways of doing things, challenge, and the big picture. Since they are attracted to theories and models, they make up the majority of those interested in personality systems, such as the MBTI and the Enneagram. Note that intuition is abbreviated "N," to distinguish it from the "I" for introversion.

ARE YOU AN INTUITIVE?

Note how many statements you agree with:

1. You think about the future more than the present or past.
2. You like systems and patterns.
3. Some of your best ideas seem to come out of nowhere.
4. Your hunches are often accurate, though the logic behind them is not always obvious.
5. You get excited about your intuition and have learned to trust it.
6. You generally prefer change to repetition.
7. Some people have trouble following your thoughts.
8. Some people think you have your head in the clouds.
9. You would rather do innovative than routine work.
10. You cannot turn your energy or enthusiasm on at will.
11. Sometimes you sense what is going to happen.
12. You are interested in the meanings of experiences, not just in the experiences themselves.
13. You like wondering and speculating and are surprised when the person you are with doesn't share this enjoyment.
14. You don't have nearly enough time to carry out all the ideas you come up with.

If most of the above statements apply to you, you are probably an intuitive type. If few of these statements apply to you, you can become more versatile by consciously developing your intuitive side.

Intuitives find unique solutions. They might realize, for example, that a circular wall could protect the city from the yearly
buffalo stampede without harming the buffalo population.
—*Nigel Thompson*

INTROVERTED INTUITIVES AT WORK   Introverted intuitives
gather information differently from sensates. They prefer focusing
on the future, imagining, and looking for underlying meanings.
Introverted intuitives' least developed and most unconscious
function is *extraverted sensation*, which may be triggered by being
overwhelmed by details or too much socializing. It often takes the
form of controlling behavior, verbal attacks, or fretting and ob-
sessing out loud.

Introverted intuitives with *thinking* (INTJs) often have
careers as engineers, attorneys, professors, computer scientists,
research scientists, business innovators and organizers, philosophers, lawyers, and computer scientists. While INTJs are primarily
introverted, it's important to realize that they also have an extraverted side. The MBTI tells us their judging function, thinking,
is extraverted. Their favorite and more introverted preference is
intuition.

If you are an introverted intuitive with thinking, appreciate
your ability to be original, visionary, and relentless. You are able
to probe subjects in depth and come up with new strategies. Your
preference for intuition may conflict with sensate employees,
bosses, or coworkers. If they have difficulty with the nonlinear
wanderings of your mind, slow down and try to explain things in
a step-by-step way. You probably function better by yourself
rather than trying to be a team player. If others see your need for
privacy as avoidance, you could explain that you do your best
work in solitude. If others complain that you ignore their opinions
and feelings, try to see things from their point of view and think of
their feelings. Tell them you can often understand people more
easily when they appeal to your thinking function. Remind your-

self, "It is neither reasonable nor productive to disregard those you work with."

Introverted intuitives with *feeling* (INFJs) often have careers as teachers, writers, artists, psychologists, psychiatrists, social scientists, clergy, librarians, charity workers, and social or ecological activists. While they are primarily introverted, the J at the end tells us that INFJs show their feeling to the world. Their feeling function is what they use to judge what they have perceived through their intuition.

If you are an introverted intuitive with feeling, appreciate your compassion, perseverance, intense inner vision, and ability to create a personal environment in the workplace. Settling on a choice that feels just right may be difficult when intuition continually brings up new possibilities. If you have a work deadline, you may have to either sacrifice the "just right" part a bit or arbitrarily cut off accepting any new possibilities, just for a while. Appreciate your idealism and your ability to bring imagination and human values to the workplace.

EXTRAVERTED INTUITIVES AT WORK Extraverted intuitives express enthusiasm for new, creative ways of doing things. The inferior function for extraverted intuitives is *introverted sensation*, which may be triggered by too much repetitive sensate work or being tired. They may become overly rigid or unrealistically obsess about something being wrong with their body.

Extraverted intuitives with *thinking* (ENTPs) often have jobs as executives, journalists, public relations consultants, photographers, psychiatrists, lawyers, politicians, entrepreneurs, scientists, computer analysts, and inventors. ENTPs argue competitively and are enterprising, competent, and innovative. They move from challenge to challenge and may be anti-authoritarian. Though they are primarily extraverted, it's important to know that they also have introversion in their personalities. The P tells us that they show intuition to the world, therefore their thinking is introverted.

Extraverted intuitives with *feeling* (ENFPs) often have jobs as teachers, journalists, artists, entertainers, clergy, and social workers. They are also found in public relations and sales. ENFPs enjoy careers where there are frequent new challenges and lots of people around. They are persuasive, idealistic, and love to meet new people. Their initial enthusiasm may fade when something new comes along. Harmony in the workplace is essential. While they are generally extraverted, their feeling function—or their valuing system—is introverted.

Thinking/Feeling

Thinkers process reality by objectively analyzing facts wherever possible, while feelers value an empathic connection with other people.

THINKING

Thinking types like facts and truth, have trouble trusting their own feelings, and sometimes suspect the feelings of others. They base their decisions on logic, focus on principles and patterns, and are critical and inquisitive.

"Thinkers might observe the needs and draw out
the plans for an entire city, including a detailed
schedule for how it will be built."
—*Nigel Thompson*

INTROVERTED THINKERS AT WORK Introverted thinkers are
most comfortable socially when given specific tasks to do and become stressed by emotional displays. After they know the facts,
they prefer to figure out what to do with them themselves. They
have the ability to think clearly and solve problems. Introverted
thinkers' least developed and most unconscious function is *extraverted feeling*. When triggered (often by too much emotion or
noise, or too little freedom), this function may produce untypical
emotional displays, distractibility, and touchiness.

Introverted thinkers with *sensing* (ISTPs) often have
jobs as mechanics and computer technicians. They're also comfortable in the military, farming, construction, and transportation
fields. While ISTPs are primarily introverted, the P at the end
points to the extraverted perceiving preference—sensing.

ARE YOU A THINKING TYPE?

Note how many statements you agree with:

1. You like to solve intellectual problems and reason things out.
2. You tend to live according to principles and laws.
3. Knowledge is one of the most important things in your life.
4. You value objectivity in others and try to be objective yourself.
5. Some people see you as too impersonal.
6. When someone tells you a personal problem, you might analyze it rather than express sympathy.
7. You do well when your ability to criticize is called for.
8. You look for fairness, balance, and truth.
9. You are methodical and notice whether others think precisely or not.
10. You like to take responsibility for making travel plans.
11. You sometimes hurt people's feelings inadvertently.
12. You tend to see things from a long-range perspective.
13. You find it difficult to be around people who don't value knowledge and logic.
14. You prefer concise, factual answers to answers that emphasize feelings.

If most of these statements apply to you, you are probably a thinking type. If few of these statements apply to you, you can become more versatile by consciously developing your thinking side.

If you are an introverted thinker with sensing, appreciate your happy-go-lucky attitude and your ability to be active, realistic, and expedient. You avoid feeling obligated, rebel from rigid routines, and are most likely anti-authoritarian. The best work situation is one with opportunities to jump in with your technical knowledge, where you can troubleshoot and have sufficient wiggle room. You prefer a career where you can be independent and make use of your practical abilities. Remember to spend some time alone to recharge.

Introverted thinkers with *intuition* (INTPs) often have jobs as computer programmers, writers, lawyers, researchers, psychologists, and scientists. (Carl Gustav Jung and Albert Einstein were probably this type.) Your intuition, or how you take in information, is extraverted—you show it to the world. You *judge* what you have intuited with your introverted thinking preference.

If you are an introverted thinker with intuition, appreciate your ability to keep the workplace interesting through being logical, skeptical, and curious. You would rather come up with ideas than carry out a course of action. Most INTPs like to search for the perfect word or perfect solutions to complex, abstract problems.

> I'm Jaqueline Girdner and I'm a mischievous thinking type. I spent my childhood in the land of imagination. Books were my friends. After years of misguided attempts to succeed in "people" places (law, business, and psychology), I remembered my friends. And I remembered the joy of being a mischievous introvert. I now kill people for a living as a mystery novelist. I have found my place in the world, and it is in my own head.

EXTRAVERTED THINKERS AT WORK Extraverted thinkers apply logic and reason to situations in the outer world and are often dominating and decisive. The inferior function for extraverted thinkers is *introverted feeling*. When triggered, often by strong emotions or being unappreciated, this preference may cause them to become illogical, have emotional outbursts, or feel tired.

Extraverted thinkers with *sensation* (ESTJs) often have careers as administrators, supervisors, lawyers, managers, insurance agents, policemen, personnel supervisors, military personnel, and sports figures. They like their workplace to be predictable and organized, take on many responsibilities, and are one of the most trustworthy, realistic, efficient, honest, and (along with ENTJs) aggressive of the types. ESTJs show their favorite preference to the world—thinking, their judging function. Sensing is secondary and introverted.

Extraverted thinkers with *intuition* (ENTJs) often have careers as lawyers, CEOs, systems analysts, executives, administrators, bankers, and industrialists. ENTJs are aggressive and make visionary leaders. They would be extremely forthcoming should the president request their advice on how to run the world, for example. Because this type is extraverted, the J represents their favorite *and* most extraverted preference (thinking). Their intuition is introverted.

FEELING

Feelers make the city human by filling it with meaning.
They integrate the environment with world views that are
continuous and supportive of a sane, balanced life.
—*Nigel Thompson*

You're fine. How am I?

Words by Clarence Thomson

Feeling types make judgments according to such values as compassion, beauty, empathic connections, and harmony. Introverted feeling types value personal experience and subjective meanings so highly, they look down upon collective opinions and the extraverts who hold them. They become inflexible when their deepest beliefs are threatened. Extraverted feeling types also have strong values and develop their ability to relate to others.

INTROVERTED FEELERS AT WORK   Introverted feelers value ideals, art, and life, and are motivated to improve the human condition. Introverted feelers' least developed and most unconscious function is *extraverted thinking*, which may be triggered by being criticized or self-criticism. It often takes the form of nit-picking or being hostile, critical, or sarcastic.

Introverted feelers with *sensation* (ISFPs) often have jobs as health care workers, medical technicians, food service workers, carpenters, teachers, bookkeepers, secretaries, nurses, physical therapists, musicians, gardeners, and artists. ISFPs are compassionate, use and take pleasure in their five senses, and tend to be good listeners. While this type is primarily introverted, its sensing is extraverted, as indicated by the P.

If you are an introverted feeler with sensation, appreciate your ability to give down-to-earth assistance, remember details, form empathic connections, and keep track of time. You like to keep the workplace pleasant, for which you like praise. Try not to

ARE YOU A FEELING TYPE?

Note how many statements you agree with:

1. You value interpersonal harmony above almost all else.
2. You have a hard time becoming interested in things that aren't personally meaningful to you.
3. You care deeply about humanity and suffer when hearing about violence.
4. You value expressing your appreciation, building trust, and healing others.
5. You naturally empathize with children and animals and stand up for those who can't speak for themselves.
6. You like to help people feel comfortable.
7. You want to be known as a loving and caring person.
8. You worry that people find you too emotional or not clear-minded.
9. Sometimes you compliment people before you've decided whether the compliment is warranted.
10. You can feel things as others feel them.
11. You are especially interested in human relationships.
12. Whatever matters to your friends and loved ones matters to you.
13. You love to have others praise you for what you have done.
14. It pains you to tell people things they don't want to hear.

If most of the above statements apply to you, you are probably a feeling type. If few of these statements apply to you, you can become more versatile by consciously developing your feeling side.

let your wish to avoid conflict get in the way of expressing your feelings. You have a caring and harmonizing nature and are especially good at working with plants, animals, and children. When something upsets you at work, instead of retreating, make a point of staying and working things out. Make sure your environment is safe for expressing what you think and feel, or you might become stressed from holding back your opinions too much.

Introverted feelers with *intuition* (INFPs) often have jobs as psychologists, artists, writers, philosophers, teachers, editors, inventors, and musicians. They are among the most idealistic and soul-searching of the types. The MBTI tells us that INFPs have both introverted and extraverted qualities—the P at the end indicates INFPs show their perceiving function, intuition, to the world.

If you are an introverted feeler with intuition, you are creative, recognize potential in others, and understand abstract, intangible aspects of life. Avoid jobs that place you in highly competitive situations. It can be helpful to know that INFP males are often gentler than most other types of males.

> The rich inner life is definitely worth all we "introverted feelers with intuition" go through. When I see a flower, a blade of grass, a Coke can, or anything else, I have a richer experience than someone whose inner life is neglected. I wouldn't give that up for anything. That's just one of many things that I love about being this type. —*Nigel Thompson, an INFP*

Honor your need for quiet and consciously use your thinking ability to determine whether you have overlooked any important facts or details. Look for opportunities in which you can engage your imagination.

> Where does one moment end and another begin? To me there are no such divisions. We attempt to freeze time but actually time is like flowing water. We say, "Here is the Mississippi River," or "Here is the Atlantic Ocean." But the water pays no mind to our silly little divisions. It flows where it will and is always in a state of oneness. Time is the same. Any divisions are artificial devices, illusions. Just ask yourself, "When does one moment end and another begin?" What can possibly separate time from itself? —*Nigel Thompson, an INFP*

EXTRAVERTED FEELERS AT WORK Extraverted feelers are good communicators, helpful, good-hearted, optimistic, encouraging, and socially talented. They act on their values, are often well organized, and tend to be conscious of social status. The inferior function for extraverted feelers is *introverted thinking*. When triggered, often by conflict or not being trusted, they may become pessimistic or depressed and withdraw.

Extraverted feelers with *sensation* (ESFJs) often have jobs as realtors, artists, secretaries, office managers, teachers, receptionists, technologists, dental assistants, speech therapists, and health professionals. They follow rules and work toward making people's lives better in a practical way. The J tells us their favorite preference, feeling, is extraverted (since their type begins with E), so we know their perceiving function, sensing, is introverted.

Extraverted feelers with *intuition* (ENFJs) often have jobs as artists, therapists, crusaders, talk show hosts, clergy, media personalities, public relations workers, and politicians. They like jobs where they can be creative and challenged. The J tells us their judging function, feeling, is extraverted, Their perceiving function, intuition, is therefore introverted.

Perceiving/Judging

The final letter in the four-letter MBTI formula, P or J, points to your most extraverted or visible personality function. Perceiving refers to how you gather information, either through sensing or intuiting it. Judging refers to how you make decisions based on that information, either through thinking (using logic or objective analysis) or feeling (based on subjectivity or empathic connection).

PERCEIVING

Perceivers easily change their minds if new information warrants it. For example, the best time for them to buy tickets to an event would be at the last moment, when it's unlikely that anything better will come along. If they use sensing, they may base their decision on whether it's going to be good weather for playing tennis instead. If they use intuition, they may base their decision on some inexplicable feeling they have at the time about whether they're really going to like that event or prefer a different event.

ARE YOU A PERCEIVING TYPE?

Note how many statements you agree with:

1. You are open-minded, look forward to change, and don't want to miss anything.
2. You are not compulsively neat or organized.
3. You go with the flow and keep your options open in the event that something more interesting might come along.
4. You often start new projects before finishing old ones.
5. You like to combine work and play.
6. You look for new information.
7. You can postpone jobs you're not interested in doing.
8. You may have conflicts with people who are uptight, but you also appreciate their ability to complete what they start.
9. You are relatively flexible and spontaneous.
10. You are receptive to trying different experiences.
11. You can see many sides of an issue.
12. You often don't mind waiting.
13. Even when you want to, you have trouble sticking to rigid routines.
14. When performing a task (cleaning the house, for example), you don't always do it in the same order.

If most of the above statements apply to you, you are probably a perceiving type.

PERCEIVERS AT WORK Perceivers have a keen eye for new information that might be useful. If you are a perceiver, appreciate your flexibility. You can be spontaneous and drop what you're doing if something else needs your attention. With your talent for picking up new information, choose an occupation where you will be valued for gathering facts or ideas. If you become stressed from too much routine and predictability, try to add variety to your job. It may not be your nature to be fastidious and orderly, so this part of work could be a challenge for you. Judgers are usually more organized and tidy than perceivers—each of you bring important assets to the workplace.

JUDGING

Judgers use either thinking or feeling to evaluate information after it has been perceived by sensing or intuition. Since they are purposeful, organized, and want to have matters settled, they might purchase tickets months ahead of an event. Thinkers may buy tickets to a play that promises to add to their knowledge and strength of character, while feelers may look for a play that prom-

ARE YOU A JUDGING TYPE?

Note how many statements you agree with:

1. You are structured and organized.
2. When things are open-ended you often feel unsettled.
3. You normally act decisively and deliberately.
4. You need to be in control of what is happening and will happen.
5. You frequently set goals and deadlines for yourself.
6. You enjoy planning and making decisions.
7. You are productive.
8. Sometimes you make your mind up too fast and regret it later.
9. You don't like clutter in your life.
10. You don't like surprises, such as people dropping in unannounced or requesting that you do something on the spur of the moment.
11. You like to complete all your work before you relax.
12. You have a reputation for being on time.
13. You have been called uptight, or you worry about being called uptight.
14. You like to have as few options to choose from as possible.

If most of the above statements apply to you, you are probably a judging type.

ises to leave them feeling good or to re-enforce their feelings about an emotional issue.

JUDGERS AT WORK   If you are a judger, appreciate yourself for being punctual, neat, and orderly. You want your decisions to be final and do not change your mind easily. You like structure and prefer clear-cut goals with as few options to choose from as possible. Try to avoid open-ended projects. Appreciate your ability to get things done. Look for an occupation where you can use your organizing and decision-making skills, rather than having to come up with raw information. You may become overly rigid in

QUIZ ON PSYCHOLOGICAL TYPES

(Answer T for "true" and F for "false")

1. Both perceiving and judging are indispensable to creativity. Perceiving helps you see possibilities, while judging helps you with carry-through.
2. Since territoriality is typical of introverts, don't invade the space around them by parking your coat on their desks.
3. Intuitive types always notice everything that's going on around them.
4. In the United States, two-thirds of men prefer their thinking function and two-thirds of women prefer their feeling function.
5. Some people, even other introverts, think of introverts as aloof and inscrutable.
6. Sensate types often have their heads in the clouds.
7. People generally favor one from each pair of sensing/intuition and feeling/thinking. If sensing is extraverted, intuition will be introverted. If thinking is extraverted, feeling will be introverted.
8. Jung devised a test for type called the MBTI.
9. Myers and Briggs observed that they were very much alike, except that one was a perceiver and the other a judger.
10. The "inferior function" refers to one's weakest preference. For example, an introverted feeler's inferior function is extraverted thinking. Since it is unconscious, it is awkward and unpredictable.
11. After Jung wrote his essays on "Psychological Types," he lost most of his interest in typology and concentrated on studying the collective unconscious.

ANSWERS:
1. true; 2. true; 3. false; 4. true; 5. true; 6. false; 7. true; 8. false; 9. true; 10. true; 11. true

your rush for closure. It is the nature of perceivers to be less orderly and neat than judgers—each of you bring important assets to the workplace.

NINE WAYS OF BEING AN INTROVERT
(AS SEEN BY THE ENNEAGRAM)

Afterword:
Napoleon Dynamite

Just listen to your heart. That's what I do.
—*Napoleon Dynamite*

In a society that caters to extraverts, the wild acceptance of the independent film *Napoleon Dynamite* is a sign that introverts may be on the brink of being liberated from their reputation as losers. Even though the quirky main character is a picked-on and socially awkward high school student, teenagers love it and are watching it over and over again. *Napoleon Dynamite* became an instant classic when it was released in 2004. An online fan club had 50,000 members almost overnight. It was a hit at the Sundance Film Festival, named Best Feature Film at the U.S. Comedy Arts Festival, and nominated for the Golden Satellite and

MTV Movie Awards. As of the spring of 2006, there were 2.25 million listings on Google for "Vote for Pedro" and other T-shirts based on the movie, and 1.7 million listings for Napoleon Dynamite dolls.

If you sat down to watch this movie expecting an explosive world conqueror, you'd be in for a surprise. Napoleon Dynamite is a grumpy-looking, slack-jawed teenager. But don't let his crabby, socially awkward demeanor fool you—he's the kind of human being you can believe in. Napoleon Dynamite is an exemplary introvert. He's not only talented and sweet, but strong and virtuous—a loyal friend, and indeed a hero. He knows who he is and he's comfortable with himself.

This movie cracks Napoleon Dynamite's poker-face facade open like an oyster and shows the world a gigantic pearl inside in terms of his generosity, inner strength, and talent. The message to non-introverts is that these secretive people might be worth taking more seriously and getting to know. Introverts may be thinking: "I feel happy and understood by this unusual and endearing movie—there are actually several fellow introverts who I can relate to!" There isn't much of a main plot but there are many subplots. Themes include tolerance, diversity, anti-materialism, and the virtue of marching to your own drummer.

Character Study

Napoleon Dynamite's director and co-writer John Hess "refuses to treat nerdiness as a disease," says Jesse Hassenger in his movie review on popmatters.com. The result is an imaginative look at a slice of life not normally seen on the big screen.

The four main introverts are Napoleon, his brother Kip, and his friends, Pedro Sanchez and Deb. Though they may be ridiculed and scorned, they are not deterred from expressing their idiosyncratic selves. The main extraverts are Napoleon's Uncle Rico and

Summer Wheatley. Even though these are fictional characters, you'll see that the Enneagram types can be applied to them.

Napoleon Dynamite's Personality

Napoleon is the "weird kid" at school, but is he oblivious to the fact or does he simply not care? He's not thinking about how he looks to others—he's more interested in playing tetherball by himself and drawing pictures of his favorite animal, the "liger" (a combination of a lion and a tiger). He tells a lot of silly lies—introverts often like to entertain themselves with whimsical humor.

In one scene, Napoleon laments his inability to attract girls because he lacks "skills, like nunchuck skills, bow hunting skills, and computer hacking skills." Napoleon might not be able to conquer the social world, but he's got the power of dynamite that movie audiences appreciate. Not to mention his many talents. I liked watching Napoleon perform the pretty song, "The Rose," in sign language with the Happy Hands Club (he's the only male member). Just for his own pleasure, he has learned how to dance from a video he had bought. Near the end of the film, Napoleon does his dance. It is a skillful, highly coordinated, graceful act of loyalty—the tour de force of the movie that wins Pedro's election for him.

Others see Napoleon as gawky. I see him as inspiring because of his ability to be true to himself, true to his friend, and sweet but understated, like when he asks in an almost monotone voice, "You guys having a killer time?"

I think Napoleon is a 9-Peacemaker in the Enneagram. There's an underlying sweetness to much of what he does, even though his exterior is a little gruff. And to take to the dance so easily implies a body-based type. When he tells Deb, "I caught you a delicious bass," at the end of the movie, we think she's a lucky girl to have caught a guy like him.

Deb's Personality

We first meet Deb and her side-ponytail when she's going door-to-door earning money for college by selling beaded key chains and other things. On Napoleon's front porch,

she apparently has a shy attack and runs off, leaving all her merchandise. Deb has a crush on Napoleon, but they are slow to connect.

I think she's a 5-Observer in the Enneagram personality system. They can be the shyest of the shy, often freeze in social situations, and are known for their ability to wear a poker face. She has a lovely smile.

Kip's Personality

Napoleon's brother, Kip, is a 32-year-old chatroom junkie who still lives at home and wears retro-sixties glasses. He's definitely a geek. When he falls in love with cyber-chick LaFawnduh, he joins Uncle Rico on a couple of scams in order raise enough cash to bring his

voluptuous soulmate to Idaho for a visit from her native Detroit. Since Kip spends most of his time searching for a soulmate, he is probably a 4-Romantic in the Enneagram system.

Pedro's Personality

Pedro Sanchez has just transferred to the school from Mexico. I think he's a 9-Peacemaker in the Enneagram system. Nines are  considered self-forgetting. This spacey, robotic kid is so clueless that he does things that could be misinterpreted as confident. He wants to take the school's most popular, attractive, and stuck-up girl to the prom, but is turned down. When he impulsively decides to run for class president against her, Deb, the shyest girl in school, and Napoleon lend a hand.

Uncle Rico's Personality

In addition to the jocks and bullies at school, Napoleon also endures slimeball Uncle Rico, who was the back-up quarterback in 1982 when Preston, Idaho, lost the state championship game. He is still trapped on the sidelines, where he was denied the chance to become an all-star quarterback when his team needed him the most. At first,  vain Uncle Rico spends most of his time videotaping his football passes and orders a time machine for traveling to his glorious past. When that doesn't work, he involves Kip in get-rich-quick schemes.

Rico is an unhealthy version of a type 3-Achiever in the Enneagram, and an extreme extravert who doesn't seem to have a thoughtful molecule in his body.

Summer Wheatley's Personality

Summer, the most popular girl in school, has a
boyfriend who looks about 35 years old and is
the biggest bully in the school. We don't
know much about either of them, except that
they are extraverts and have typically extraverted values. The boyfriend is especially
adept at sneering at those who don't observe the
social rules. This is a good place to mention the
rest of the student body. There's another bully
who occasionally slams a nerd into a locker and
tries to steal one of the nerd's bikes. To me, the student body represents those people who normally go
along with the status quo or society—the extraverts. But in this
case, they change their minds and vote for the introvert.

In a way, it doesn't seem like the extraverted characters of
Rico and Summer—and her awful bullying boyfriend—are the vil-
lains here as much as what they represent about our society.

A segment of the American public is finally ready to admire someone who doesn't care about fitting in, but instead is able to stay
true to himself, as Napoleon Dynamite does. For this outsider, life
isn't about being popular or beautiful. Just like introverts the
world over, Napoleon marches to his own drummer, and his inner
greatness shines when the time is right.

Appendix
Introverts/Extraverts at Their Best and Worst

At Their Best

Introverts (as experienced on the inside) . . .

1. are skillful listeners and observers.
2. are thoughtful, able to focus, and good at concentrating.
3. are self-contained; they want to be liked but don't go to extremes worrying about how they appear to others.
4. can make space for someone who doesn't feel included.
5. form lasting connections and are loyal to their friends.
6. are good company for themselves; they explore facts, feelings, and/or how things work.
7. notice subtleties and have a long attention span.

Extraverts (as experienced on the inside) . . .

1. easily fit into many kinds of social situations and enjoy having many friends.
2. are energetic and accomplish a lot.
3. know how to present themselves and network.
4. infect others with their enthusiasm.
5. communicate information and/or feelings well.
6. are confident about their own abilities.
7. can be assertive when necessary.

Introverts (as seen from the outside, especially by extraverts) . . .

1. are sensitive listeners and loyal friends.
2. set a good example of being able to concentrate and focus.

3. are self-contained and independent.

4. have a deepening influence on groups.

5. are steady and have a calming and stabilizing effect on others.

6. are good observers of social dynamics and/or laws of nature.

7. are insightful and/or empathic.

Extraverts *(as seen from the outside, especially by introverts)* . . .

1. have good rapport and bring people together.

2. are enthusiastic, lively, and uninhibited; they can be active from morning 'til night.

3. have a definite image of how they want to be seen.

4. are entertaining; they have a lot to talk about on account of their breadth of experiences and interests.

5. express their feelings well.

6. are up-front about what's on their minds.

7. know how to get things done.

At Their Worst

Introverts *(as experienced on the inside)* . . .

1. are too sensitive, shy, and/or quiet to feel comfortable socially; they often feel left out.

2. expect others to take action for them.

3. are uncertain about the acceptable way to act or look.

4. need to feel engaged to feel alive when with others, yet have trouble connecting with people and/or translating their thoughts into words.

5. have trouble expressing themselves, especially in large social gatherings; they feel flustered when cornered or pressured and worry that they might lash out in anger or frustration.

6. don't tell people what's on their minds, especially if it might lead to conflict.

7. feel vulnerable, insecure, and easily overwhelmed; they are sometimes too shy or frightened to be effective.

Extraverts *(as experienced on the inside):*

1. worry about rejection.

2. overpower others with their energy.

3. become anxious about how they appear to others.

4. are afraid to be alone and/or to live without plans.

5. suffer when they're not the center of attention.

6. need to bluster their way through embarrassment when they haven't taken the time to check out all the information.

7. have a short attention span; they feel empty when under-stimulated and sometimes are afraid to stop talking.

Introverts *(as seen from the outside, especially by extraverts)* . . .

1. get tired of being around other people; they drop out to be by themselves when the extraverts are still having fun.

2. can't keep up with extraverts in "doing" situations (shopping, attending sports events, parties).

3. don't know how to present themselves; appear awkward, uncomfortable, standoffish, unfriendly, snobbish, and/or aloof.

4. are poor at complementing and apologizing; they may deliver a lecture instead of participating in the conversation.

5. withhold from fear and/or cruelly blurt out their "truth."

6. don't tell people what they're thinking or don't respond fast enough.

7. are oddballs or nerdy and hard to figure out.

Extraverts *(as seen from the outside, especially by introverts)* . . .

1. want all the attention and expect or demand applause.

2. require too much stimulation; they fill every moment with activity.

3. please the crowd; they compromise their values in order to gain acceptance.

4. are automatically positive, especially feeling types, because they think that's what others like.

5. are showy, loud, or obnoxious; they take up more than their share of time talking, emoting, or throwing their power around.

6. do not persevere long enough to get in touch with their true feelings or thoughts.

7. rely on society's values instead of questioning them and figuring out their own.

Endnotes

CHAPTER 1: THE INTROVERT IN AN EXTRAVERTED WORLD

1. Sunyata (Emmanuel Sorensen), *Sunyata*, ed. and comp. Betty Camhi and Elliott Isenberg (Berkeley, CA: North Atlantic Press, 1990).

2. Anne Brennan and Janice Brewi. *Celebrate Midlife, Jungian Archetypes and Mid-life Spirituality* (New York: Crossroad Press, 1988).

3. Allen L. Hammer and Wayne D. Mitchell, "The Distribution of MBTI Types in the United States," *The Journal of Psychological Types* 37 (1996).

4. Sunyata (Emmanuel Sorensen), *Sunyata*, ed. and comp. Betty Camhi and Elliott Isenberg (Berkeley, CA: North Atlantic Press, 1990).

5. John Boe, "Life Itself," *Life Itself, Messiness Is Next to Goddessness and Other Essays* (Wilmette, IL: Chiron Publications, 1994).

6. John Boe, "The Introvert in Shakespeare," *Life Itself, Messiness Is Next to Goddessness and Other Essays* (Wilmette, IL: Chiron Publications, 1994).

7. Elaine N. Aron, *Highly Sensitive People* (New York: Broadway Books, 1996).

8. Jane Mayer, *The New Yorker*, 12 October 1998.

CHAPTER 2: RELATIONSHIPS

1. Anthony Storr, *Solitude, A Return to the Self* (New York: Balentine Books, 1988).

2. Michele Laroque, actress (*The Closet*), in a *San Francisco Chronicle* article by Bob Graham, 2 July 2001.

CHAPTER 3: PARENTING AND TEACHING CHILDREN

1. C. G. Jung, *Memories, Dreams, and Reflections* (New York: Vintage Books, 1965).

2. Anthony Storr, *Solitude, a Return to the Self* (New York: Ballantine: 1988).

3. Frank J. Sulloway, *Born to Rebel, Birth Order, Family Dynamics, and Creativity* (New York: Pantheon Books, 1996).

4. Diana Walsh, "Children Learning Game of Friendship," *San Francisco Chronicle*, 14 April 2002.

5. Interview with Charlie Rose on *Charlie Rose Show*, KQED (PBS), 6 September 2001.

6. Sunyata (Emmanuel Sorensen), *Sunyata*, ed. and comp. Betty Camhi and Elliott Isenberg (Berkeley, CA: North Atlantic Press, 1990).

CHAPTER 4: ABOUT ADOLESCENTS

1. Quote by D. Gentry (1989 audio tape) from Richard Frankel's *The Adolescent Psyche—Jungian and Winnicottian Perspectives* (London: Routledge, 1998).

2. Sunyata (Emmanuel Sorensen), *Sunyata*, ed. and comp. by Betty Camhi and Elliott Isenberg (Berkeley, CA: North Atlantic Press, 1990).

3. Shankar Vedantam, "Researchers Theorize Brain Changes Are Linked to Behavior," *Washington Post*, 3 June 2001.

4. Richard Frankel, *The Adolescent Psyche—Jungian and Winnicottian Perspectives* (London: Routledge, 1998).

CHAPTER 5: CREATIVITY

1. Robert Engman, from Stanley Rosner and Lawrence E. Abt, editors, *The Creative Experience* (New York: Grossman Publishers, 1970).

2. George Nelson, from Stanley Rosner and Lawrence E. Abt, editors, *The Creative Experience* (New York: Grossman Publishers, 1970).

3. Isaac Bashevis Singer, from Stanley Rosner and Lawrence E. Abt, editors, *The Creative Experience* (New York: Grossman Publishers, 1970).

4. Mihaly Csikszentmihaly, *Flow, The Psychology of Optimal Experience* (New York: Harper Perennial, 1990).

5. A. Alvarez, "The Playful Pianist," *The New Yorker*, 1 April 1996.

6. Gerhard Adler, quoted in June Singer's *Boundaries of the Soul, the Practice of Jung's Psychology* (Garden City, NY: Doubleday, 1972).

7. Selden Rodman, from Stanley Rosner and Lawrence E. Abt, editors, *The Creative Experience* (New York: Grossman Publishers, 1970).

8. A. Alvarez, "The Playful Pianist," *The New Yorker*, 1 April 1996.

9. June Singer, *Boundaries of the Soul, the Practice of Jung's Psychology* (Garden City, NY: Doubleday, 1972).

10. Richard Rees, *Simone Weil: A Sketch for a Portrait* (Carbondale: Southern Illinois University Press, 1966).

11. Paul Saltman, from Stanley Rosner and Lawrence E. Abt, editors, *The Creative Experience* (New York: Grossman Publishers, 1970).

12. Sidney Lumet, from Stanley Rosner and Lawrence E. Abt, editors, *The Creative Experience* (New York: Grossman Publishers, 1970).

13. Mihaly Csikszentmihaly, *Flow, The Psychology of Optimal Experience* (New York: Harper Perennial, 1990).

14. Alice Calaprice, *The Quotable Einstein* (Princeton, NJ: Princeton University Press, 1996).

15. Robert Engman, from Stanley Rosner and Lawrence E. Abt, editors, *The Creative Experience* (New York: Grossman Publishers, 1970).

16. Arthur Koestler, from Stanley Rosner and Lawrence E. Abt, editors, *The Creative Experience* (New York: Grossman Publishers, 1970).

17. Aaron Copland, from Stanley Rosner and Lawrence E. Abt, editors, *The Creative Experience* (New York: Grossman Publishers, 1970).

18. Bonnie Cashin, from Stanley Rosner and Lawrence E. Abt, editors, *The Creative Experience* (New York: Grossman Publishers, 1970).

10. Jean Shioda Bolen, *Crossing to Avalon* (San Francisco: HarperSanFrancisco, 1994).

20. Bonnie Cashin, from Stanley Rosner and Lawrence E. Abt, editors, *The Creative Experience* (New York: Grossman Publishers, 1970).

21. Sidney Lumet, from Stanley Rosner and Lawrence E. Abt, editors, *The Creative Experience* (New York: Grossman Publishers, 1970).

22. Paul Saltman, from Stanley Rosner and Lawrence E. Abt, editors, *The Creative Experience* (New York: Grossman Publishers, 1970).

23. W. Novak and Moshe Waloks, *The Big Book of Jewish Humor* (New York: Harper Perennial, 1990).

24. C. G. Jung, *Memories, Dreams, and Reflections* (New York: Vintage Books, 1965).

CHAPTER 6: DR. CARL GUSTAV JUNG AND INTROVERSION/EXTRAVERSION

1. C. G. Jung, *Memories, Dreams, and Reflections* (New York: Vintage Books, 1965).

2. Same.

3. Same.

4. Dr. Anthony Stevens, *Archetypes, A Natural History of the Self* (New York: Quill, 1983).

5. June Singer, *Boundaries of the Soul, The Practice of Jung's Psychology* (Garden City, NY: Doubleday, 1972).

6. Carl Gustav Jung, *Aion, Part II, volume 9, The Collected Works of C. G. Jung* (Princeton, NJ: Princeton University Press, 1958).

7. June Singer, *Boundaries of the Soul, The Practice of Jung's Psychology* (Garden City, NY: Doubleday, 1972).

8. Anne Brennan and Janice Brewi, *Celebrate Midlife, Jungian Archetypes and Mid-life Spirituality* (New York: Crossroad Press, 1988).

9. Same.

10. Edward Guthmann, "Lucas Says Media Spreads Inaccuracies Like a Virus," *San Francisco Chronicle*, 2 February 2000.

11. C. G. Jung, *Memories, Dreams, and Reflections* (New York: Vintage Books, 1965).

CHAPTER 7: NEUROLOGY AND PERSONALITY

1. Dr. Jerome Kagan, professor of developmental psychology, Harvard University. Heard on *The Infinite Mind: Shyness*, NPR radio, the week of 26 December 2001.

2. A. Furnham and L. Strbac, "Music is as distracting as noise," *Ergonomics*, 20 February 2002.

3. Robert Lee Hotz, "Neuroscientists Mine the Depths of Emotions," *Los Angeles Times*, 8 November 2002.

4. Dr. Jerome Kagan, professor of developmental psychology, Harvard University. Heard on *The Infinite Mind: Shyness*, NPR radio, the week of 26 December 2001.

5. B. R. Strelow and W. B. Davidson, "Introversion-extroversion, tempo, and guided imagery," *Psychological Reports*, April 2002.

6. S. K. Opt and D. A Loffredo, "Communicator image and Myers-Briggs Type Indicator extroversion-introversion," *Journal of Psychology*, November 2003.

7. K. Nakao, J. Takaishi, K. Tatsuta, H. Katayama, M. Iwase, K. Yorifuji, and M. Takeda, "The influences of family environment on personality traits," *Psychiatry and Clinical Neurosciences*, February 2000.

8. S. Ferracuti and A. De Carolis, "Relationships among Eysenck's extroversion, Rorschach's Erlebnistypus, and tolerance of experimental tonic pain (Cold Water Pressor Test)," *Perceptual and Motor Skills*, February 2005.

9. Y. Bar-Haim, "Introversion and individual differences in middle ear acoustic reflex function," *International Journal of Psychophysiology*, October 2002.

10. A. J. Young and J. L. Walters, "Relationship between daily heard improvement production values and Myers-Briggs type indicator as a measure of management ability," *Journal of Dairy Science*, August 2002.

11. Daniel Goleman, *Emotional Intelligence* (New York: Bantam Books, 1995).

12. James Newman, Ph.D., "The Neurophysiology of Extraversion-Introversion," unpublished paper, 7 May 1984.

13. Joseph LeDoux in "Taking a Clinical Look at Human Emotions" by Claudia Dreifus, *New York Times*, 8 October 2002.

14. Jeffrey Kluger, "Secrets of the Shy," *Time*, 4 August 2005.

15. S. K. Opt and D. A. Loffredo, "Communicator image and Myers-Briggs Type Indicator introversion-extroversion," *Journal of Psychology*, November 2003.

16. E. B. Bookman, R. E. Taylor, L. Adams-Campbell, and R. A. Kittles, Department of Genetics and Human Genetics, Howard University, Washington, D.C., and National Human Genome Center at Howard University.

17. From the Human Genome Project Information website: www.orni.gov/hgmis/medicine/genetherapy.html.

CHAPTER 8: INTROVERTS, THE WORKPLACE, AND MYERS–BRIGGS

1. Albert Einstein, *The Quotable Einstein*, comp. Alice Calaprice (Princeton, NJ: Princeton University Press), 1996.

Index

Q

R

Other Books from Ulysses Press

THE 7 HEALING CHAKRAS: UNLOCKING YOUR BODY'S ENERGY CENTERS
Brenda Davies, M.D., $14.95

The 7 Healing Chakras explores the essence of chakras—vortices of energy that connect the physical body with the spiritual.

A CHORUS OF WISDOM
Edited by Sorah Dubitsky, Ph.D., $14.95

Essays from over 25 visionary thinkers that offer insight and revelation in a manner that is sure to bring positive change.

HOW MEDITATION HEALS: A SCIENTIFIC EXPLANATION
2nd edition, Eric Harrison, $14.95

In straightforward, practical terms, *How Meditation Heals* reveals how and why meditation improves the natural functioning of the human body.

JESUS AND BUDDHA: THE PARALLEL SAYINGS
Marcus Borg, Editor   Introduction by Jack Kornfield, $14.00

This book traces the life stories and beliefs of Jesus and Buddha, then presents a comprehensive collection of their remarkably similar teachings on facing pages.

PORTABLE REIKI: EASY SELF-TREATMENTS FOR HOME, WORK AND ON THE GO
Tanmaya Honervogt, $14.95

Presents do-it-yourself, step-by-step treatments for quick, effective Reiki healing—anytime, anyplace. The book's system is specially designed to help busy people release stress, improve health and restore personal energy.

PSYCHIC SHIELD: THE PERSONAL HANDBOOK OF PSYCHIC PROTECTION
Caitlín Matthews, $14.95

Psychic Shield provides simple and commonsense strategies for overcoming negative thinking, dealing with difficult people, becoming attuned to spiritual guidance, and protecting one's inner peace.

SECRETS OF THE PEOPLE WHISPERER: A HORSE WHISPERER'S TECHNIQUES FOR ENHANCING COMMUNICATION AND BUILDING RELATIONSHIPS

Perry Wood, $12.95

The author shows how the same techniques for developing trust and understanding with a horse can work equally well in one's personal, business, family, and romantic relationships.

SENSES WIDE OPEN: THE ART & PRACTICE OF LIVING IN YOUR BODY

Johanna Putnoi, $14.95

Through simple, accessible exercises, this book shows how to be at ease with yourself and experience genuine pleasure in your physical connection to others and the world.

STOP LIVING YOUR JOB, START LIVING YOUR LIFE: 85 SIMPLE STRATEGIES TO ACHIEVE WORK/LIFE BALANCE

Andrea Molloy, $12.95

A successful personal life coach shows how to identify priorities, make meaningful decisions and take specific actions.

WHAT WOULD BUDDHA DO?: 101 ANSWERS TO LIFE'S DAILY DILEMMAS

Franz Metcalf, $9.95

Much as the "WWJD?" books help Christians live better lives by drawing on the wisdom of Jesus, this "WWBD?" book provides advice on improving your life by following the wisdom of another great teacher—Buddha.

To order these books call 800-377-2542 or 510-601-8301, fax 510-601-8307, e-mail ulysses@ulyssespress.com, or write to Ulysses Press, P.O. Box 3440, Berkeley, CA 94703. All retail orders are shipped free of charge. California residents must include sales tax. Allow two to three weeks for delivery.

Acknowledgments

I thank Nigel Thompson for sharing his ideas on the MBTI and the Enneagram. Other friends/psychologists who contributed include Elizabeth Ratcliffe, Annemarie Sudermann, John Weber, and Catherine Valdez. I also learned from Renee Baron.

I thank my introverted husband Gus for being ever-patient when I asked him questions and for providing some of the quotations.

I thank the Center for the Application of Psychological Type for sending articles and books. I'd like to draw particular attention to *The Experience of Introversion: An Integration of Phenomenolical, Empirical, and Jungian Approaches* by Kenneth J. Shapiro and Irving E. Alexander.

I thank Mary Beth Crenna, Penny deWind, Gail Wread, Harriet Glaser, Karen McArdle, Harry Gans, Karen Costarella, Mary Porter-Chase, Lee Friedman, Harriet Whitman Lee, Elaine Chernoff, Jaki Girdner, Steve Kresge, Phil Gerrard, Joyce Burks, Fran Foltz, Carolyn Rhodes, Greg Booi, Knute Fisher, Kirby Olson, Joan Ryan, Shirley Caputo, Arlette Schlitt-Gerson, Tom Rosin, Bob Pool, Don Kyle, my children and their partners, and my grandchildren for our discussions and letting me observe them.

I thank the many other introverts and extraverts I interviewed.

My editors at Ulysses Press, Claire Chun and Lily Chou, offered wise suggestions and were a pleasure to work with.

—Elizabeth

About the Author

Elizabeth Wagele, author of *The Enneagram Made Easy*, *Are You My Type, Am I Yours?*, *The Enneagram of Parenting* and *Finding the Birthday Cake*, has spent a lifetime studying the differences in personality types. She traces the roots of her keen interest in personality type back to junior high school, when she was extremely curious about the differences she observed in students and teachers. Her work now focuses on the Enneagram system of nine personality types and the Myers-Briggs Type Indicator (MBTI) personality system. Also a musician, Elizabeth released a CD, *The Enneagram of Beethoven*, on which she talks about Beethoven's personality and music and plays from his piano sonatas. She is currently illustrating a book on parenting using "brain styles" by Susie Weller. Elizabeth, mother of four and grandmother of five, lives in Berkeley, California, with her husband Gus. For more information, visit www.wagele.com.